A. Lagueux

A. Lagueux14@Gmail.com

A.Lagueux@yahoo.com

# Citrus and Spice

## A year of flavour

## SYBIL KAPOOR

Photography by Patrice de Villiers

SIMON &
SCHUSTER

LONDON • NEW YORK • SYDNEY • TORONTO

First published in Great Britain by Simon & Schuster UK Ltd, 2008
A CBS Company

Simon & Schuster UK Ltd
1st Floor, 222 Gray's Inn Road, London WC1X 8HB

1 3 5 7 9 10 8 6 4 2

Design: Two Associates
Food photography: Patrice de Villiers
Styling: Lucy Harvey and Cath Roddick
Home economy: Bridget Sargeson, Janice Murfitt

Printed and bound in China

ISBN 978-1-84737-221-5

# CONTENTS

*For Raju, with love*

# ACKNOWLEDGEMENTS

Every book I have ever written has taken on a life of its own, and this book is no exception. I am deeply grateful to the many people who have helped to bring *Citrus & Spice* to life. In particular, I would like to thank my brother Julian Polhill and his partner Lucy Copeman, as it was their inspired present that first gave me the idea. I would also like to thank Rosemary Scoular and Chris Cope at United Agents for their unfailing support and Janet Copleston at Simon & Schuster for choosing to publish the book. My editor Paula Borton has been a dream to work with, as has David Eldridge of Two Associates, whose design has perfectly captured the book's mood.

A special thank you goes to Patrice de Villiers. She has translated my thoughts and recipes into stunningly beautiful photographs to create a unique cook book. Thanks too, to Bridget Sargeson and her family A-team of Jack and Stella, who made all the recipes look gorgeous; to Janice Murfitt, for stepping in when needed; to Lucy Harvey and Cath Roddick and to the hard working but always cheerful Marie Absolom, Patrice's assistant.

My grateful thanks to Heston Blumenthal for finding the time when he had none, and to Monica Brown for all that she has done. Thanks too, to Sophie Grigson, who kindly allowed me to use her mother's recipe for celery soup; as well as to Nicki Lampon for her meticulous editorial work and to Selfridges for finding lemon verbena when none was to be had. Last, but not least, a big thank you to my mother and, of course, to my ever supportive, much loved husband, who is a constant source of inspiration.

# FOREWORD BY HESTON BLUMENTHAL

I am often asked whether I am a cook/chef, a scientist or an artist. Firstly, I am a professional cook and therefore a chef. I am not a scientist but embrace science as a tool in my cooking and whilst it might sound a little conceited to describe myself as an artist, I would say that if man can use paints, brushes and canvas to generate an emotional response, then so too can cooks with food.

Eating is the only thing that stimulates all of the senses and this, if nothing else, should explain the incredible potential that food and our surroundings have for generating emotion. At the heart of this is our memory; we all live in our own sensory worlds and whilst some key elements of food desire are hard wired (the need for fat and sugar for example), most food preferences are born from nurture; memories generated from life's experiences. The sense of smell, for example, is now known to be the most powerful memory trigger of all the senses and although very personal, there are still smells that many of us can relate to. The smell of a Douglas fir is enough to bring back that sense of childhood excitement at Christmas, or the first smell of freshly cut grass signifying the onset of summer. When this is paired with the noise of a lawnmower, it can become even more wonderful.

In addition to smell and sound triggers, there are other mechanisms now known to influence our food preferences. Context, learned associations and rewards are three such examples. Why does Muscadet, sipped on the banks of the Loire on a summer's day taste so good with fresh oysters, only to find the same wine when brought back home tastes tart and insipid? It's not the wine that has changed but the context in which it was served.

Reward mechanisms can significantly heighten our love for a food. We just have to look at the difference between pistachios in the shell compared to ones that have already been shelled. A cup of steaming hot chocolate given to us after a long cold walk can seem that much more satisfying. Ice cream became my ultimate food reward from childhood when my grandmother, on a Sunday morning, dragged myself and my sister around the bric a brac stalls in Church Street market. The only thing that kept us going through these times of hardship was the trip to Regents snack bar on the Edgware road on the way home. This traditional award-winning Sicilian ice cream parlour seemed like an oasis. With its over-sized, plastic ice cream cone over the door and larger-than-life Sicilian servers in their white coats, this place was like a scene from a mafia film. I watched in awe as they trowelled vanilla and coffee ices into tubs before carefully pressing the lid, sliding them into a brown paper bag and handing them over to us. This ice cream tasted fantastic. In part because of the anticipation and delayed gratification but above all, this was a reward on the most delicious scale.

Even a fruit as seemingly humble as a tangerine can conjure the most wonderful memories. The learned association of tangerine and Christmas time is such a powerful one that even today, whenever I peel one of these little beauties and catch the aromas of the oils being sprayed into the air, memories of waking up on Christmas morning to see the stocking at the end of my bed are as vivid as if they were happening today.

*Citrus & Spice* by Sybil Kapoor exemplifies all that is exciting about the modern approach to food and cooking. Sybil combines scientific knowledge with the pure emotional wonderment that food and cooking can bring and does so in such a delicious way both in her recipes and through her text.

This is a book to savour in every sense and indeed every sense is explored. Her recipes are delightful and are packed with ideas and tips that will inspire every level of cook.

HB

# 'Scent forms part of our memory. It shapes our taste and ultimately defines who we are.'

For centuries, cooks, chefs and writers have spilled much ink in an attempt to instruct their readers in the art of cooking. The reader, in turn, has been subjected to practical manuals, recipe-led travelogues, culinary manifestos, scientific works and even the odd satire – all in the interest of culinary art. Yet it seems to me that the nature of cooking itself is changing. Today, everyone craves constant gustatory excitement and an emotional response to food. It is time for a fresh approach.

At the heart of all good food lies one magic element – flavour. And by flavour, I mean smell – the scent of food that we experience before and during eating. It is flavour that can make the difference between something tasting ordinary and being irresistible. It is flavour, in other words smell, that instantly links us to memories and associations, which in turn influence our mood and shape our perception of what we're eating. Modern cooking depends on understanding and interpreting the resonances between the world around us and the food we eat.

Creating sublime dishes is all about experiencing life. Everything that we eat consists of taste, flavour, texture, temperature and colour. The five tastes – bitter, sweet, salty, sour and umami – are the building blocks of recipes, while texture, temperature and colour will, to some degree or other, affect our perception of the dish. However, it is flavour that evokes the most powerful emotional reaction.

Since the terms flavour and taste are often interchangeable, it is important to understand the difference. The easiest way to do this is to crush a bay leaf and sniff. It will release a sweet green fragrance, the delicate flavour of a creamy béchamel sauce. Now, take a tentative bite. You will discover that it tastes repulsively bitter. In other words, it is the smell of the bay leaf rather than its taste that flavours food.

Every time you add a flavour to a dish, you are adding your own associations and emotional reactions. Even more importantly, you are provoking them in your guests. If their emotions are positive, their perception of your food will be coloured by their mood and it will seem twice as good. Consider walking into a house filled with the scent of a blackberry crumble baking in the oven. Its jammy smell may instantly evoke a sense of comfort that makes you relax and feel happy, spoilt and hungry (provided, of course, that you like blackberry crumble).

Naturally, such a dish tastes twice as good as one you haven't smelt cooking.

Memory and emotion are integrally linked to identity. I have a pretty friend who will sip lemon verbena tisane and nibble sweet grapes when we meet for coffee and cake. Her life is structured around eating the healthiest, most natural ingredients she can find. I cannot imagine her ever eating a gooey chocolate cake, let alone a flapjack. Her attitude and choice of food is part of her personality and part of her charm.

From the moment you are born you start to sniff, taste and react to the world around you. Layer upon layer of smells and their associations are built upon, giving you, as a cook, an incredible repertoire of flavours to play with in your recipes. Scent instantly conveys season, weather, time and place. A sprig of mint dropped into a pan of boiling new potatoes will enhance the subtle sweetness of the cooked potatoes, but it will also add myriad unconscious associations and their attendant moods.

In this book I will show you how to identify the different flavours and, hopefully, help you to consider what they might mean to you by highlighting what they mean to me. This will allow you to add your own emotional resonances to every dish that you cook and to create food that is uniquely your own. It will also allow you to create dishes that are utterly irresistible, since you should be able to generate similar reactions in your guests.

According to flavourists, there is an infinite number of smells. However, that does not mean that we shouldn't attempt to categorise them. Wine buffs do it all the time, and a good cook needs order to create a fine-tasting dish. So, I have divided this book into 12 categories of flavour, but there are many others. The aim is to reawaken your sense of smell. Sniff everything! After all, the whiff of a wet dog can influence your opinion on how to use a mature cheese in a recipe as much as the sweet aroma of freshly picked mushrooms.

I've arranged these flavour chapters to resonate with the changing months of the year, as seasonality is integral to my cooking. The zesty scent of a freshly cut grapefruit conjures up the icy cold culinary minimalism of January as surely as the heady smell of honeysuckle evokes sultry June nights eating raspberries and cream in the garden.

Within each chapter I've explored how that particular group of flavours can influence our perception of food. The recipes in each chapter illustrate how that category of flavour works with ingredients from that month. My choices are inevitably subjective and occasionally idiosyncratic, but I hope that they will open up a new culinary world where you are acutely aware of flavour and the emotional reaction it can engender. Such knowledge frees the cook to create wonderful food.

SK

# JANUARY *CITRUS*

## PEELING AN ORANGE

Cooking is a form of alchemy, and like any alchemist you have to understand your base ingredients. Each type of flavour will produce different associations and responses to your food. Citrus notes, perhaps more than any other flavour, add excitement to food. The icy freshness of a lemon cuts through cloying marinades to make meat taste sweet and fresh in the depths of winter, just as the complex aroma of a pomelo adds a peppery floral edge to pomegranate seeds in a January fruit salad. For me, citrus flavours symbolise the stark simplicity of the New Year, mingled with a feeling of anticipation that comes with a new beginning; whether it is a slice of lemon dropped into a gin and tonic or lemon grass crushed under my knife for a hot and sour soup.

For many there is the added pleasure of abstention after the decadence of Christmas. Somehow, the fresh clean aroma and sour taste of citrus fruit epitomises this feeling of virtue. The tingle of grapefruit zest in a citrus chilli dressing on a salmon carpaccio and rocket salad inevitably makes a guest feel as if they are being restrained and virtuous, which ensures that they enjoy the meal all the more.

Over the years, my desire for simplicity in food has increasingly led me to pare back the ingredients in my recipes so that the intense taste and flavour of my chosen citrus fruit can sparkle within them. Obviously, you need good quality ingredients to cook in this way, otherwise there is a risk that the citrus flavours will show up any weakness in the other ingredients. I've always had a secret suspicion that complicated recipes were originally designed to disguise poor quality food. Thus fine white beans, good olive oil, red onion and chilli need nothing more than fresh lemon juice to taste gorgeous. Add some lightly seared tuna, a few romaine leaves and a wedge of lemon, and suddenly Italian lemon groves and the sparkling sea can be experienced in the cool wintry light of a British kitchen. Heaven on a plate.

## BATAVIA, ORANGE AND TARRAGON SALAD

The natural fragrance of the orange segments in this salad lifts the mood with its pure fresh flavour.

**SERVES 4**

**2 large oranges**

**2 Batavia lettuce hearts**

**1 bunch watercress, washed and cut into sprigs**

**1 tablespoon tarragon leaves, ripped**

**2 tablespoons extra virgin olive oil**

**salt and freshly ground black pepper**

Using a sharp knife, cut away the pith and peel of the oranges. Holding each fruit over a bowl to catch the juice, cut away each segment so that they drop into the bowl, leaving behind the fibrous casing. Squeeze any excess juice from the casing into the bowl. Add the inner leaves of the lettuce, sprigs of watercress and ripped tarragon leaves.

Season the salad with the olive oil, salt and freshly ground black pepper. Gently mix and serve.

## SEARED SCALLOPS WITH LEMON SOY SAUCE

One of the easiest ways to capture citrus flavours is to use citrus zest in your cooking. This contains the essential oils that are widely used in food flavourings. In this recipe, lemon zest is briefly infused into a soy honey dressing.

**SERVES 6**

**1 Thai chilli, finely sliced**

**6 tablespoons Kikkoman soy sauce**

**2 tablespoons honey**

**finely grated zest and juice of 2 organic or unwaxed lemons**

**2 tablespoons toasted sesame oil**

**24 large scallops**

**3 tablespoons extra virgin olive oil**

Put the chilli in a small saucepan with the soy sauce and honey. Set over a low heat and stir until the honey has dissolved. Remove from the heat and add the lemon zest, sesame oil and 2 tablespoons lemon juice.

Prepare the scallops by removing the tough small white muscle. Slice each scallop in half. If your scallops were sold with their roes, leave these attached to one half of the scallops as you clean and slice.

Preheat an oven-top griddle pan. Once very hot, oil the scallops and place on the griddle. Cook for about 1½ minutes per side. Divide the scallops between six plates. Whisk the tepid sauce and spoon on to the scallops.

## SEVILLE ORANGE MARINATED CHICKEN

There was a time when British cooks would use sour Seville oranges throughout the winter months in much the same way as they now use lemons. Their zest has an intense fragrance. Today Seville oranges are only sold in Britain during the latter half of January and the very beginning of February, so if you can't find any, follow the adaptation notes in this recipe. Serve with the Batavia, orange and tarragon salad (see page 13).

**SERVES 4**

**8 sprigs lemon thyme**

**1 shallot, sliced**

**2 tablespoons extra virgin olive oil**

**juice of 1 Seville orange or 3 tablespoons orange juice mixed with**
    **2 tablespoons lemon juice**

**4 organic chicken breasts, skinned**

**salt and freshly ground black pepper**

**For the orange butter:**

**55 g unsalted butter, softened**

**1 Seville orange or 1 orange and ¾ tablespoon lemon juice**

**salt and freshly ground black pepper**

Roughly rip the leaves of the lemon thyme and place in a mixing bowl with the shallot and olive oil. Add the juice of a Seville orange or 3 tablespoons ordinary orange juice mixed with 2 tablespoons lemon juice.

Take the chicken breasts, remove the fillets and trim off any discoloured flesh. Add the fillets to the marinade and place each breast between two sheets of cling film. Using a rolling pin carefully flatten each breast into a thin escalope. Remove from the cling film and mix into the marinade. Cover and chill for 30 minutes.

Meanwhile, make the orange butter by beating together the butter and the finely grated zest of a Seville or normal orange. Then beat in either 1½ tablespoons Seville orange juice or ¾ tablespoon ordinary orange juice and ¾ tablespoon lemon juice. Season to taste. Place on some greaseproof paper and gently roll into a cylinder. Chill until needed.

Shortly before serving, preheat an oven-top griddle pan over a medium heat. Remove the chicken from the marinade. Lightly season and grill for about 3–4 minutes on each side or until cooked through. Slice the butter and leave to melt on top of each chicken breast.

## STIR-FRIED BEEF WITH LIME LEAVES AND CHILLI

Citrus flavours can also be found in other foods such as kaffir lime leaves and lemon grass. You need fresh kaffir lime leaves for this recipe, as freeze-dried lime leaves don't retain sufficient fragrance to impart their flavour. Fresh kaffir lime leaves can usually be found in Chinese and Thai supermarkets.

**SERVES 2**

200 g rump steak, trimmed weight

1 teaspoon sunflower oil, plus 3 tablespoons

1 tablespoon Kikkoman soy sauce

1 tablespoon Thai fish sauce

1 teaspoon caster sugar

2 kaffir lime leaves, very finely sliced

½ red pepper, deseeded

115 g green beans, trimmed

1 teaspoon peeled and finely julienned fresh ginger

1 clove garlic, finely chopped

1 red Thai chilli, finely sliced

Trim the steak of any fat. Cut into fine matchsticks and mix in 1 teaspoon sunflower oil. Set aside. In a small bowl, mix together the soy sauce, fish sauce, caster sugar, lime leaves and 3 tablespoons water. Set aside.

Cut the red pepper into similar-sized strips as the beef. Finely slice the green beans at a slight angle.

When you are ready to eat, set a non-stick frying pan or wok over a high heat. Add the 3 tablespoons sunflower oil and, as soon as it is sizzling hot, add the ginger and garlic. Stir fry for a few seconds, or until they start to turn golden, then immediately add the chilli, followed by the beef. Stir fry briskly for a few more seconds then, as soon the meat begins to colour, remove to a bowl with a slotted spoon, leaving the oil and juices in the pan. Add the green beans and red pepper, stir fry for a few seconds, then return the meat with any juices and immediately mix in the soy sauce mixture. Bring up to the boil and serve immediately with steamed rice.

# VENISON WITH PORT AND ORANGE SAUCE

Citrus aromas are often classified as a top note in perfumery. They are instantly perceived but fade quite quickly, which makes them an ideal flavouring when you want to add light freshness to a rich savoury dish, such as here. This sauce takes around 50 minutes to make from start to finish, so prepare in advance. It also tastes good with seared duck breasts.

**SERVES 4**

**1 orange**

**4 black peppercorns**

**350 ml red wine, such as cabernet shiraz or pinot noir**

**500 ml good chicken stock (see page 168)**

**100 ml port**

**1 tablespoon redcurrant jelly**

**salt and freshly ground black pepper**

**4 x 170 g venison steaks, trimmed weight**

**3 tablespoons extra virgin olive oil**

Begin with the sauce. Using a potato peeler, finely pare the zest from the orange and place in a saucepan with the peppercorns and red wine. Set over a high heat and boil until the wine has reduced to a few tablespoons. Add the stock, return to the boil and cook briskly until it has reduced by at least three quarters.

Squeeze the juice from the orange and mix into the stock with the port and redcurrant jelly. Continue to boil until the sauce has reduced a little and tastes good. You should have about 300 ml. Strain and set aside.

Shortly before serving, reheat the sauce. Season the steaks. Set a non-stick frying pan over a high heat, add the oil to the pan and, once hot, fry the steaks for 2–3 minutes on each side or until medium rare. Remove the steaks and serve with the hot sauce.

## PAPAYA, LIME AND MINT SALAD

Citrus fruit has fragrance in both its juice and zest. Here, the fresh floral aroma of the lime juice plays with fruit and herb notes in the salad, while its sour taste enhances the sweetness of the papaya. A dish that makes you feel virtuous and spoilt at the same time.

**SERVES 6**

**3 ripe papayas**

**4½ tablespoons lime juice**

**1 small bunch mint**

**2 bunches watercress,**
   **trimmed and washed**

**400 g white Belgian endive**

**3 tablespoons extra virgin olive oil**

**salt and freshly ground black pepper**

Peel the papayas and halve lengthways. Neatly scoop out and discard the seeds, then slice across the width of each half. Place in a large mixing bowl with the lime juice.

Strip the mint leaves from their stems and roughly rip. Add to the papaya with the watercress sprigs. Unfurl the Belgian endive leaves and cut each leaf in half. Mix into the salad with the olive oil, season to taste and serve.

## VODKA GRAPEFRUIT SYLLABUB

The fragrant zing of grapefruit is normally associated with an energising breakfast or a refreshing starter. However, a clever cook will use this natural association to create a pudding that both surprises and delights the eater by its unexpected nature.

The perfect foil to grapefruit's intense citrus flavour is cream, whether it is in the form of a syllabub, mousse or ice cream. If you wanted to play on these flavours further, serve this syllabub with a delicate sweet and sour rhubarb jelly.

**SERVES 6**

**2 white grapefruit**

**6 tablespoons vodka**

**6 tablespoons caster sugar**

**565 ml double cream**

Using a julienne zester, remove the zest from the grapefruit in tiny strips. Set aside.

Squeeze the juice from one grapefruit and place in a large mixing bowl with the vodka and caster sugar. Add the cream and whisk until it forms soft floppy peaks. Gently fold in the grapefruit zest and, if necessary, adjust the sweetness to taste. Cover and chill until needed. When ready to serve, spoon into six wine glasses.

# RHUBARB, POMEGRANATE AND POMELO COMPOTE

Pomelo has a light floral citrus fragrance that can add an intriguing complexity to both sweet and savoury salads. The layering of different sour tastes in this recipe has the happy effect of making the eater feel healthy, regardless of whether you serve the compote for breakfast or pudding.

**SERVES 4**

**400 g forced rhubarb, trimmed**

**185 g caster sugar, or to taste**

**1 pomegranate or 150 g fresh pomegranate seeds**

**1 pomelo**

Use rhubarb stems that are of a similar thickness, otherwise they will cook at different rates. Trim the rhubarb into even bite-sized chunks and place in a wide saucepan with the sugar and 3 tablespoons water. Cover and set over a very low heat, stirring occasionally until the sugar has melted. This will take about 10–15 minutes if the water doesn't simmer. Allow the rhubarb to barely simmer for a further 4 minutes. It should have just lost its crunch but still hold its shape.

Meanwhile, cut the pomegranate in half and scoop out all its juicy seeds into a large bowl. Using your fingers, carefully detach any seeds that are still attached to the bitter-tasting pale yellow fibrous casing. Discard the casing. One pomegranate will yield more seeds than a 150 g packet but use them all, they taste so good.

Cut the top and bottom off the pomelo. Cut away its thick pith and skin by slicing down its sides from top to bottom. You will be left with an orb of glistening peeled fruit. Hold this above the pomegranate seeds and, with a serrated knife, cut the segments away from their casing so that they drop into the bowl. Squeeze the empty casing over the bowl to ensure that you release all its juice. Sometimes pomelos are full of seeds – just pull them out before adding the segments to the pomegranate.

Tip the hot rhubarb into the pomelo and pomegranate. Mix thoroughly and serve once cool.

# MARMALADE

Open a jar of marmalade and you will release the intense flavour of Seville oranges. It's a smell that evokes the happiness of student breakfasts and instils a deep sense of optimism when combined with the aroma of coffee and buttered toast.

**MAKES 2 KG**

**1.225 kg organic Seville oranges**

**1.7 litres water**

**1.4 kg granulated sugar**

**1 heaped teaspoon black treacle**

Wash all the fruit and place in a large pan with the water. Cover tightly, bring to the boil and simmer gently for 1½ hours or until the fruit is very soft and easily pierced with a knife.

To sterilize your jam jars, wash in soapy water, rinse in very hot water and dry in a moderate oven. Alternatively, wash in the dishwasher, then slightly open the door and leave to steam dry. Turn the screw lids upside down to drip dry.

Transfer the fruit to a bowl, leaving the cooking liquid in its pan. Once the fruit is cool enough to handle, slice it in half and scrape out the pulp, pips and most of the pith into the pan, making sure that the pulp is thoroughly mashed up. Bring back to the boil and reduce by half before straining into a jam pan. This takes about 20 minutes.

Meanwhile, slice all the fruit skins into thin or thick strips – depending on your taste – and add to the jam pan. Clip a jam thermometer on to the side of the pan and return to the boil before mixing in the sugar and black treacle. Stir the sugar until it has completely dissolved, then increase the heat and vigorously boil the marmalade until it reaches setting point – 106°C. This will take about 5 minutes. If you don't have a thermometer you can test if it is ready by dropping a tiny spoonful of marmalade on to a chilled saucer. As it cools, a skin will form. If this wrinkles when gently pushed, the setting point has been reached.

Once the marmalade has reached setting point, remove from the heat and leave to sit for 10 minutes, stirring occasionally to distribute the peel evenly. Pour into warm, dry, sterilized jam jars, cover with waxed paper discs, waxed side down, and seal. Label and date if you are so minded.

# FEBRUARY OZONE

## CLAMBERING OVER ROCK POOLS

Ozone is the scent of the sea. It is the saline fragrance
that is momentarily experienced on lifting the lid of a
bowl of piping hot miso soup or biting into a crisp
crab beignet. It is the most ephemeral of flavours and
carries with it a sense of freedom. The sort of freedom

you feel when walking on a windswept beach where sky, sea and sand melt into one another.

Once in the warmth of the kitchen it becomes harder to relate to this elusive, wild flavour. Perhaps this is partly due to the fact that the fresh ozone aroma of some foods can change into a lingering quayside smell that takes a lot of scrubbing to eliminate. Think poached kipper pans. However, such reservations should be swept aside in favour of the intense pleasure experienced on smelling fresh sea air. Open a packet of dried seaweed, pour on some water and suddenly an energising briny aroma fills the kitchen and makes your heart skip a beat with excitement. Toss spaghetti with some buttery chilli garlic clams and you will find yourself dreaming about Venice floating in the winter mist.

As you might expect, ozone is found in marine-related foods, ranging from shellfish and seaweed to salt-water fish and marsh plants such as samphire. Many of these, such as scallops, kelp and dried bonito flakes, are also rich in umami and salt. Used in moderation, these two tastes will add a moreish element to dishes, making them seem extra good. Umami also enhances the natural sweetness in food, so many ozone-flavoured ingredients will benefit from a hint of sourness to prevent them from becoming cloying. Try cooking the Grilled sea bass on page 29 with and without the kelp and then eat it with and without a squeeze of lemon and you will see what I mean.

Treated plainly and with a light hand, ozone-flavoured food is the perfect medium for inducing a carefree feeling. Simply prepared, its fragrance appears natural and in keeping with the emotion it engenders. Some lightly grilled prawns brushed with a peppery young virgin olive oil, or a sprinkling of mixed dried seaweed flakes in the greenest of salads, will hint at the sea. Perfect for lifting your mood on a cold February day.

# CRAB BEIGNETS

The delicate ozone flavour of the crab is released when you bite into these crisp soft-centred beignets, which can be served as a starter or canapé. For canapés, drop half a teaspoon of mixture into the oil and cook for 3 minutes – this makes 80 canapés.

**SERVES 8 AS AN APPETISER**

**150 g white crab meat**

**115 g cold unsalted butter, diced**

**salt**

**115 g plain flour, sifted**

**4 medium eggs, roughly beaten**

**55 g finely grated Gruyère**

**a large pinch of cayenne pepper**

**freshly ground black pepper**

**corn oil for deep fat frying**

Pick through the crab meat and remove any tiny pieces of shell. Gently squeeze any excess moisture from the meat and set it aside.

To make the choux pastry base, pour 300 ml cold water into a small saucepan. Add the diced butter and a pinch of salt. Bring to a brisk boil and, once the butter has melted, remove from the heat and tip in the sifted flour. Return to a low heat and, using a wooden spoon, beat vigorously for 3 minutes or until the mixture is glossy and leaves the side of the saucepan. Remove from the heat and gradually beat in the eggs, a little at a time. Make sure each bit of egg is absorbed into the paste before adding the next. Once the paste is smooth and glossy, beat in the cheese and cayenne pepper, quickly followed by the crab meat. Season to taste. If you wish to set the mixture aside at this stage, press some cling film over the paste's surface and chill.

Heat the oil in a deep fat fryer to 180°C. When you are ready to serve, first dip a teaspoon into the hot oil to prevent the mixture sticking to the spoon, then drop a teaspoonful of mixture into the hot oil so that it forms a ball. Repeat the process, taking care not to let the beignets stick together. Once you have enough to cook comfortably without the temperature dropping, fry for 5 minutes or until golden brown, crisp and light. Flip them over half way through the cooking time to ensure that they are evenly cooked.

Remove from the oil, shake off the excess and tip on to a tray lined with kitchon paper. Repeat the process until all the beignets are cooked. Sprinkle with salt and serve with a leafy salad.

## FRESH OYSTERS WITH MINT, LIME AND CORIANDER RELISH

Oysters taste of the sea. I've combined them here with citrus and herbal flavours to evoke a sense of spring. If you plan to shuck (open) the oysters yourself, you will need a special oyster knife. Buy a few extra oysters if you feel in need of practice. You can always eat the rejects. Some fishmongers will shuck them for you, but you will need to collect them shortly before needed and transport them very carefully so as not to lose their saline juice from their shells. Keep them chilled.

**SERVES 4**

**3 tablespoons lime juice**

**1 tablespoon Thai fish sauce**

**1 shallot, finely sliced**

**½ tablespoon finely shredded fresh ginger**

**½ green Thai chilli, finely sliced**

**½ teaspoon caster sugar**

**a large handful fresh mint leaves**

**a large handful fresh coriander leaves**

**24 oysters, opened**

Place the lime juice and Thai fish sauce in a small mixing bowl. Add the shallot, ginger, chilli and caster sugar. Very roughly chop the mint and coriander leaves and mix into the relish. Set aside while you prepare the oysters. If you want to prepare the relish quite far in advance, do everything apart from the final chopping and mixing of the leaves so that they retain their fragrance and bright colour.

To shuck the oysters, wrap your left hand in a tea towel to guard against slipping and place an oyster in the palm of your bound hand. Reverse this process if left-handed. The curved side of the oyster should nestle in your palm. Place the blade of the oyster knife under the hinge and push it into the oyster. Then, firmly holding the top of the shell with the fingers of your left hand, lever the blade of the knife up and twist slightly to force the two shells apart. Discard the flat top shell. Finally, cut underneath the oyster to free it from its curved shell. Try not to spill its precious juices.

Arrange the oysters, on ice if you wish, and serve with the relish.

## KIPPER PASTE

The smoky briny flavour of kippers instantly evokes breezy holidays on the British coast. This is a very spicy kipper paste, so if you only like a hint of chilli, just add a small pinch of cayenne pepper. It is gorgeous eaten with hot white toast or spread on to homemade Oat cakes (see page 44). For the ultimate toasty flavour, make Melba toast (see page 128). Serve with cornichons.

**SERVES 6**
**3 kippers (at least 200 g each)**
**85 g unsalted butter, softened**
**2 tablespoons lemon juice**
**½ teaspoon cayenne pepper**
**50 ml double cream**
**salt to taste**

Place the kippers in a large saucepan. Cover with just-boiled water and set over a high heat. As soon as the water begins to boil, remove from the heat and leave for 3 minutes before draining the kippers into a colander.

Once cool enough to handle, pull away the bones and extract the succulent flesh from the skin of each kipper. This is quite fiddly as kippers possess a lot of fine bones, but it is well worth the effort. In fact the main problem lies in not eating all the kipper before you've finished flaking it. You need about 200 g cooked kipper flesh. Cover and chill until cold.

Place the butter and lemon juice in a food processor. Add the cayenne pepper according to your taste. Process until a soft fluffy butter forms, then add the cold kipper flakes and whiz once more until barely smooth. Lastly, add the cream and process until smooth. Don't over process or it can take on a glue-like texture. Adjust the seasoning to taste and transfer to a sealed container. Chill until needed.

## GRILLED SEA BASS WITH KELP

Dried kelp, *Laminaria longicruris*, or kombu as it is called in Japan, is a magic ingredient when it comes to cooking. It is rich in iodine, which adds a hint of ozone flavour, and glutamic acid, which imbues food with an intense savoury, umami taste. You'll see what I mean if you cook this simple recipe. This fish tastes absolutely wonderful. It needs no further seasoning other than a hint of lemon. Try serving with the Chips on page 133 and a simple green salad.

**SERVES 4**

**4 x 15 cm-lengths dried kombu**

**1 tablespoon sake**

**4 x 450 g line-caught or farmed sea bass, filleted**

**2 tablespoons extra virgin olive oil**

**1 lemon, quartered**

Place the dried kombu on a large plate and gently rub the sake into its leathery leaves. Leave to soften for 10 minutes.

Cut three angled slashes into the skin of each sea bass fillet. Place a piece of softened kombu on to the flesh of the first fillet and sandwich the second fillet flesh side down on to the kombu. Repeat with the remaining fillets. Set aside for 20 minutes and no longer.

Preheat an oven-top griddle pan over a medium-high heat for 5 minutes. Discard the kombu and gently rub the fish in 2 tablespoons olive oil. It needs no further seasoning. Grill flesh side down for 3–4 minutes or until seared with golden marks, then flip over and cook for a further 3 minutes or until cooked through. Serve with the lemon quarters.

# BUCKWHEAT NOODLES WITH NORI

Nori is made from dried laver, *Porphyra umbilicalis* – a small-leaved, red seaweed that grows extensively across the world. It adds an addictive ozone note to these noodles and will ensure that you feel virtuous and healthy as you slurp them up. Nori sheets are sold in different sizes, but you need about 7.5 g for this recipe. The noodles are served at room temperature.

**SERVES 2**

**2 teaspoons finely chopped fresh ginger**

**2 tablespoons sake**

**2 tablespoons Kikkoman soy sauce**

**2 tablespoons mirin**

**6 spring onions**

**170 g Japanese soba (buckwheat) noodles**

**100 g peeled, cooked North Atlantic prawns**

**1 teaspoon plus 2 tablespoons toasted sesame oil**

**2 medium eggs, beaten**

**½ tablespoon sunflower oil**

**7.5 g toasted nori sheets**

Put the ginger, sake, soy sauce and mirin in a small saucepan. Set over a low heat and slowly bring up to a simmer, then cook for 2 minutes. Leave to cool while you prepare the other ingredients.

Trim the spring onions and finely slice their pale green stems. Place in a large mixing bowl. Gradually add the noodles to a pan of unsalted boiling water, making sure that it doesn't stop boiling. Cook according to the packet instructions until al dente. This is usually about 5–7 minutes. Drain and rinse thoroughly under the cold tap.

Meanwhile, pat the prawns dry on kitchen paper and mix into the spring onions. Set a non-stick frying pan over a high heat. Whisk a teaspoon of sesame oil into the eggs. Add ½ tablespoon of sunflower oil to the pan and, once hot, add the beaten eggs and cook as a thin omelette. Fry for 2 minutes or until cooked through. Tip out and, as soon as it is cool enough to handle, roll up and finely slice. Mix into the prawns.

Snip the nori into small pieces and add to the prawns with the well-drained noodles. Whisk 2 tablespoons sesame oil into the soy dressing and mix into the noodles. Serve immediately.

## CARRAGEEN ALMOND CREAM PUDDING

Carrageen or Irish Moss, *Chondrus crispus*, is a reddish-purple seaweed that grows on the sea-splashed rocks of the lower shoreline. In Britain it was traditionally used as a type of gelatine in wobbly milk puddings. It imparts a light ocean flavour to food. This can be served with lightly poached apples, pears or plums.

Dried carrageen can be bought online from the Spanish food importer, Delicioso. For further information see www.delicioso.co.uk or phone 01865 340055.

**SERVES 4**

**10 g dried carrageen**

**750 ml Gold Top full fat milk**

**2 organic lemons**

**115 g caster sugar**

**½ –1 teaspoon almond extract**

Rinse the carrageen thoroughly, then place in a bowl and cover with cold water. Leave to soak for 15 minutes, then snip off and discard the tough stems and any discoloured leaves.

Place the milk in a heavy-bottomed saucepan. Finely pare three strips of zest from one of the lemons and add to the milk with the seaweed. Simmer for 30 minutes then strain into a bowl and mix in the sugar. Finely grate the zest from the remaining lemon and mix into the milk. Add the almond extract to taste. Pour into a pretty serving bowl and, once cool, chill until set.

# RICH CHOCOLATE NORI ICE CREAM

The iodine flavour of nori tastes amazing with bittersweet chocolate. It needs to be left for a good 12 hours for the flavour to develop, so you might as well make it a day or two before you need it.

**SERVES 8**

**200 g granulated sugar**

**5 medium organic egg yolks**

**200 g Valrhona Caraïbe or other good dark chocolate**

**250 ml full fat milk**

**250 ml double cream**

**2 sushi nori sheets (about 6 g)**

Measure 100 ml water into a small heavy-based saucepan and add the sugar. Clip a jam thermometer on to the side of the pan. Set over a medium heat and stir occasionally until the sugar has dissolved, then bring up to the boil and boil vigorously until the mixture reaches 120°C, or hard ball stage. This will take about 5–7 minutes.

Meanwhile, using a hand-held electric whisk, beat the egg yolks in a heatproof dish until thick and creamy. As soon as the sugar syrup reaches 120°C, turn the electric whisk to its highest setting and pour a thin, slow stream of the just-boiled syrup into the egg yolks as you whisk. The egg yolks will gradually expand into a thick pale creamy mousse – keep whisking until it is really thick. Set aside.

Break the chocolate into a large bowl and set it over a large pan of just-boiled water. Stir occasionally until the chocolate has melted. You may need to replace the hot water once. Meanwhile, put the milk and cream into a saucepan and bring up to just below boiling point. It should be just a little hotter than the chocolate. Using a wooden spoon, stir the hot milk into the chocolate bit by bit. As it becomes amalgamated, add more milk. Once all the chocolate is melted into all of the milk, transfer to a jug and chill in the fridge.

Using a pair of scissors finely cut the nori into tiny (grape pip-sized) fragments. Once the chocolate is tepid, mix in the nori and whisk the mixture into the egg mousse. Some of the nori will stick to the whisk, but scrape it off and return it to the mixture. Pour into your ice cream machine and churn according to the manufacturer's instructions. Alternatively, pour into a shallow container, freeze and, after the first hour, beat with a fork every 40 minutes or so to ensure it has a smooth texture.

MARCH EARTH

## FRESHLY DUG POTATOES

The scent of earth runs deep in our psyche. A hint of rain-splashed muddy vegetables or damp fallen leaves can evoke a primeval sense of oneness with nature, but too strong a whiff can trigger revulsion with its closeness to foul smells. Earth is a flavour group that requires careful handling to ensure a positive response. Simplicity and moderation are essential. The fragrant earthy flavour of a jacket potato, for example, is strangely comforting with its rough baked skin and childhood connotations of campfires, wood smoke and fresh air.

The more you start to sniff out earthy flavours, the more you find. Oats, barley and buckwheat all have soft earth-like tones, as do many pulses such as lentils and black beans. Root vegetables are also a rich source of earthy notes, ranging from the intensely caramel-like aroma of sweet potatoes to the fresher flavour of celeriac. Perhaps the primitve appeal of such foods lies in their starchy nature. Emotionally, there is no difference between digging up and munching a raw pignut, *Conopodium majus*, and eating a perfectly steamed Jersey Royal potato. Both induce a feeling of peace and contentment.

Earth is a category of flavour that leads the cook into the fascinating, but rarely discussed, area of modern experimental cooking, where environment is translated into food. Imagine eating a culinary interpretation of a Potato Field or Lava and Ice. These are two dishes by René Redzepi, chef owner of Noma in Copenhagen. The former is a potato purée with a sprinkling of earthy flavoured, crunchy, dried malt crumbs, while the latter is a reduced beetroot juice scattered with tiny cubes of smoked marrow jelly and sour shards of a buttermilk horseradish ice. Colour, texture, temperature, taste and flavour are all used to interpret the Nordic wilds. Both leave the eater feeling rooted in a wintery landscape.

This school of cooking might seem far removed from the domestic cook, but in reality we all take ingredients and marry them with others as a direct result of our interpretation of the world around us. To many rural Britons, the scent of a simmering potato, onion and celery soup evokes the sharp smell of freshly dug soil on a windswept March day. Its pale colour hints at the muted tones of a British landscape emerging from winter. Add to this soft, pebble-like Oat rolls (see page 45) and a sharp-toned British blue cheese, and subconsciously you will begin to create an impression of a spring day with its violets, gushing streams and shaded frost pockets.

# CELERY SOUP

There are certain recipes that it is hard to beat, and this is one of them. It comes from one of the first cook books I owned, Jane Grigson's *Good Things* (1971). Her ratio of onion and potato to celery creates a subtle-tasting soup, while the dried dill adds a wonderful peppery edge to the earthy flavour of the celery and potato. This is gorgeous eaten with Oat rolls (see page 45) and Wigmore blue cheese.

**SERVES 4**

**3 tablespoons extra virgin olive oil**

**340 g outside sticks celery, finely diced**

**170 g onion, finely diced**

**170 g peeled potato, finely diced**

**1 teaspoon dried dill**

**1 litre good quality chicken stock**

**100 ml thick double cream**

**For the garnish:**

**100 ml double cream**

**a handful celery leaves**

Place a large heavy-bottomed saucepan over a medium heat. Add the oil and, once hot, stir in the diced vegetables and dried dill. Cover and sweat for 15 minutes or until the vegetables are soft and tender. Add the stock, bring up to the boil and simmer for 20 minutes or until everything is meltingly soft.

Purée and strain into a clean saucepan. Add the cream, season to taste, adding more dill if necessary. Reheat when ready to serve and add a swirl of cream to each bowl. Top with a celery leaf or two and serve.

## WARM LENTIL SALAD

The wide variety of earth-flavoured foods available allows the cook to play with different tones to create a satisfying whole. In this salad the earthy tones of the lentils resonate with those of the green beans and carrots, while the celery, herbs and Feta introduce fresher, more verdant notes that hint at spring.

---

**SERVES 4**

**200 g puy lentils**

**1 bay leaf**

**1 teaspoon smooth Dijon mustard**

**1 clove garlic, finely diced**

**2 tablespoons white wine vinegar**

**6 tablespoons extra virgin olive oil**

**a handful parsley leaves, finely chopped**

**1 bunch chives, finely sliced**

**salt and freshly ground black pepper**

**150 g fine green beans, trimmed**

**1 carrot, peeled and finely diced**

**2 inner sticks celery, finely diced**

**115 g barrel-cured Feta**

**1 Castel franco lettuce or salad leaves
   of your choice**

**1 lemon, quartered**

Wash the lentils and place in a saucepan with the bay leaf and 700 ml water. Bring up to the boil, cover and simmer for 35 minutes or until the lentils are tender but still holding their shape. The time and amount of water needed will depend on the age and dryness of the lentils. Newly harvested dried lentils will take nearer 25 minutes.

Meanwhile, whisk together the mustard, garlic, vinegar and olive oil in a large bowl. Add the herbs and season to taste.

Bring a second pan of unsalted water to the boil. When the lentils are nearly cooked, drop the beans into the boiling water and cook for 7 minutes or until tender. Remove the beans with a slotted spoon and leave to drain. Then add the diced carrot and celery to the boiling water. Leave for 1 minute – roughly the time it takes to return to the boil, then drain, shake thoroughly and mix into the vinaigrette.

Once the lentils are tender but not sludgy, tip into a strainer, remove the bay leaf and leave to drain for 5 minutes.

Slice the beans into small rounds and add to the vinaigrette along with the warm lentils. Mix thoroughly and season to taste. Crumble the Feta into the salad. Divide the lettuce between four plates, spoon on the salad and serve with lemon wedges.

## JERUSALEM ARTICHOKE AND BACON SALAD

Earthy-flavoured foods have a tendency to be cloying, since they also tend to be quite starchy. The simplest way to negate this is to combine them with fresh flavoured or piquant tasting ingredients. Jerusalem artichokes taste amazingly sweet but are an acquired taste – hence the recipe for two.

**SERVES 2**

**500 g Jerusalem artichokes, scrubbed clean**

**1 tablespoon lemon juice**

**1 tablespoon white wine vinegar**

**5 tablespoons extra virgin olive oil**

**1 clove garlic, finely chopped**

**1 small bunch parsley, leaves finely chopped**

**salt and freshly ground black pepper**

**200 g lean back bacon**

**3 tablespoons pine nuts**

**a handful wild rocket**

**1 batavia heart, separated**

Peel the Jerusalem artichokes, cutting off any knobbly bits as you do so. Cut into 2-cm chunks and place in a bowl of cold water with the lemon juice until you are ready to steam them. Place in a steamer and cook for about 6–8 minutes or until tender.

In a large mixing bowl, whisk together the vinegar with 3 tablespoons olive oil, the garlic and chopped parsley. Season to taste and mix in the warm cooked Jerusalem artichokes.

Meanwhile, trim the bacon of fat and cut into squares. Set a non-stick frying pan over a high heat and, once hot, add 2 tablespoons olive oil, followed by the bacon. Fry briskly for 3 minutes or until the bacon begins to turn crisp. Drain on some kitchen paper to remove the excess oil, then mix into the artichokes.

Place the pine nuts in a small dry saucepan. Set over a low heat and toast the nuts, shaking regularly until they are golden and fragrant. Tip into the artichoke salad.

In a separate bowl mix together the salad leaves. Divide the undressed leaves between two plates. Spoon the warm artichoke salad on to the salad leaves and serve immediately.

# ROAST LAMB WITH HORSERADISH BEETROOT

'Comfort food' in Britain often refers to some form of intense-tasting meat and root dish, such as shepherd's pie or roast beef and parsnips. Perhaps its highly nutritional content originally introduced such emotions to our ancestors, as they roasted wild meat over an open fire while baking foraged roots in its ashes. Whatever the reason, earthy flavoured root vegetables induce a sense of security when eaten with meat.

Fresh horseradish root is often sold in the weeks before Easter due to its appearance on the Seder tray at Passover. It should be peeled before grating. However, some supermarkets also sell jars of plain grated horseradish in their sauce section. This should be kept refrigerated once opened. This meal tastes wonderful with spinach.

**SERVES 4**

**500 g raw beetroot**

**2 plump, French-trimmed racks of lamb**

**1 clove garlic, finely chopped**

**2 tablespoons extra virgin olive oil**

**salt and freshly ground black pepper**

**3 tablespoons crème fraîche**

**1 tablespoon freshly grated horseradish**

**2 large handfuls parsley leaves, finely chopped**

Preheat the oven to Gas Mark 6/200°C. Wash the beetroots under the cold tap, twist off their leaves and place the roots in a pan of cold water. Cover and bring to the boil. This will take about 10–15 minutes. Cook briskly, uncovered, for 30 minutes, or until the roots feel tender when pierced with a knife. The time will vary depending on the size of the beetroots.

Meanwhile, trim the lamb of excess fat and sinew. Place in a roasting tray. Rub with the garlic and olive oil, season and place in the centre of the preheated oven. Roast for 20 minutes for medium rare, then remove and leave to rest in a warm place for 10 minutes before carving.

While the lamb is cooking, make the sauce for the beetroot. Mix together the crème fraîche, freshly grated horseradish and finely chopped parsley. Season to taste. As soon as the beetroot is cooked, drain and top and tail. Peel off the skin using kitchen paper to protect your hands from the heat. Cut the beetroot into segments and mix into the crème fraîche. It will turn a shocking pink. Serve warm with the lamb, pouring any meat juices from the roasting pan over the sliced lamb.

## BAKED POTATOES WITH SAFFRON MAYONNAISE

Potatoes, perhaps more than any other vegetable, taste of the earth, especially some of the older varieties, such as the aromatic Shetland Black or British Queen. As a result the unwitting eater will feel grounded and content.

**SERVES 6**
**6 medium potatoes**
**a pinch of saffron threads**
**salt**
**3 tablespoons white wine vinegar**
**2 medium organic egg yolks**
**freshly ground black pepper**
**300 ml groundnut oil**
**sea salt, to serve**

Preheat the oven to Gas Mark 5/190°C. Scrub the potatoes clean and stab in several places with a sharp knife. Place in the centre of the preheated oven and bake until tender. The time will vary according to the size of the potato. Egg-sized potatoes take around 45 minutes, while medium potatoes should cook within an hour.

Place the saffron in a small bowl with a pinch of salt and grind into a powder using the back of a teaspoon. Warm the vinegar in a small non-corrosive saucepan over a low heat. Pour over the saffron and leave until tepid.

Place the egg yolks in the smaller bowl of a food processor. Season with freshly ground black pepper. Whiz briefly, then add the saffron vinegar and blend together. Begin adding the oil slowly, drop by drop, until the mixture begins to form an emulsion, then increase the flow of liquid to a steady dribble. The mayonnaise will form a thick sauce by the time you've finished adding the oil. Season to taste and chill, covered, until needed.

Once the potatoes are cooked, remove and cut a cross in their tops. Using a tea towel, grasp the bottom of the first potato and squeeze from the base to open up the cross. Repeat with the remaining potatoes. Serve with sea salt and the mayonnaise.

# PARSNIP CAKE WITH CINNAMON BUTTER ICING

One of the great pleasures of consciously cooking with flavours is that you start to explore how a particular flavour group might work in a different context. It seemed to me that if carrots taste good in cakes, then so too should the more aromatically earthy parsnip. Unusually, this cake batter does not contain any fat. Nevertheless, it is moist and unbelievably light.

**SERVES 12**

**1 lemon**

**1 orange**

**250 g small parsnips, peeled**

**270 g unblanched hazelnuts**

**50 g plain flour, sifted**

**1 teaspoon baking powder**

**a pinch of salt**

**2 teaspoons ground cinnamon**

**50 g walnuts, roughly chopped**

**5 medium eggs, separated**

**200 g unrefined caster sugar**

**100 g full fat cream cheese**

**200 g icing sugar**

**55 g unsalted butter, melted and tepid**

Preheat the oven to Gas Mark 4/180°C. Lightly oil a 25-cm round cake tin with a removable base. Line the sides and base with lightly oiled baking paper.

Finely grate the lemon and orange and place the zest in a mixing bowl with 1 tablespoon lemon juice and 1 tablespoon orange juice. Set aside a further tablespoon of each juice for the icing. Roughly grate the parsnips – including their cores. Mix into the citrus zest and set aside.

Place the hazelnuts and flour in a food processor and whiz in short bursts until the nuts are ground finely. Tip into a bowl and mix in the baking powder, salt, 1 teaspoon of cinnamon and the walnuts.

Place the egg whites in a large dry bowl. Whisk until the they form soft peaks. Add 2 tablespoons unrefined caster sugar and continue to whisk, gradually adding the remaining sugar until it is all added and the egg white forms a glossy, floppy meringue.

Roughly beat the egg yolks. Fold them into the egg whites with a metal spoon, followed by a third of the flour mixture, then a third of the parsnips. Repeat until all the ingredients are mixed into the meringue. Pour into the prepared cake tin and bake in the middle of the oven for about 35 minutes or until the cake springs back when pressed and an inserted knife comes out clean.

Remove from the oven. Once cold, remove from the baking tin and peel off the paper. Wrap in foil and chill for 2 hours.

Using a wooden spoon, beat together the cream cheese, icing sugar and remaining 1 teaspoon of cinnamon. Add the reserved lemon and orange juice, then beat in the butter. Spread the icing all over the cake and chill until firm. Decorate with a few hazelnuts.

## OAT CAKES

Ground and rolled oats have a mellow earthy flavour, which can be used to advantage if you want to introduce an earthy element to other dishes. You can either cook them in Oat rolls (see opposite), in which case they will also have a wild yeasty note, or bake them in oat cakes, to which they will add a toasty earthy tone. Both are good eaten with blue cheese, pâtés and soups.

**MAKES 14 BISCUITS**
**sunflower oil for greasing baking sheets**
**225 g medium oatmeal**
**2 tablespoons plain flour, plus extra for rolling**
**½ teaspoon salt**
**½ teaspoon bicarbonate of soda**
**½ tablespoon melted butter**

Preheat the oven to Gas Mark 5/190°C. Lightly grease two baking sheets with oil. In a bowl, mix together the oatmeal, 2 tablespoons flour, salt and bicarbonate soda. Stir in the melted butter and enough warm water (about 100 ml) to form a firm dough. Turn out and lightly knead for 2 minutes or until the mixture forms a smooth dough. If it breaks up, it needs a little more water. Don't worry, just stick it back in the bowl, add a tablespoon or so of water and knead vigorously before trying again.

Lightly sprinkle the work surface with flour and thinly roll out the dough. Take a 7-cm scone cutter and stamp out the oat cakes. Place on the baking tray. Knead together the trimmings and repeat the process until you have used up all the dough. Bake in the preheated oven for about 10 minutes. The oat cakes are cooked when they are lightly coloured and crisp. Cool on a cake rack and store in a biscuit tin.

# OAT ROLLS

To appreciate the delicate yeasty flavour of these rolls, serve still warm from the oven with a good unsalted butter. Alternatively, try serving with an earthy flavoured soup such as Celery soup (see page 37).

**MAKES 10 ROLLS**

**2 teaspoons dried yeast**

**150 g mixed grain malthouse flour**

**200 g strong white flour**

**150 g medium oatmeal**

**1 teaspoon salt**

**20 g rolled oats for topping**

Sprinkle the yeast into 100 ml tepid water. Leave for 10 minutes or until the yeast has dissolved, smells lovely and looks active. Mix together the two flours, oatmeal and salt. Add the yeast water, rinse the yeast bowl with approximately 200 ml tepid water and gradually mix it into the flour to make a soft, sticky dough. Water quantities can vary with different flours.

Knead the dough on a clean surface for 10 minutes or until it feels smooth and elastic. It will become less sticky as it is kneaded.

Place the dough in a large mixing bowl. Cover with cling film and leave for 3 hours in a warm, draught-free room or until the dough has doubled in size.

Put the rolled oats into a small bowl. Turn the dough out, briefly knead and divide into 10 equal-sized pieces. Roll each piece into a round bun, then firmly press the top into the rolled oats and slightly flatten before placing on a non-stick baking sheet. Lightly cover with a clean tea towel and leave to rise for 45 minutes or until well risen and puffy. Preheat the oven to Gas Mark 7/220°C.

Remove the towel and bake the rolls in the preheated oven for 15 minutes or until lightly coloured. Cool on a cake rack.

## BUCKWHEAT PANCAKES WITH APPLES AND CALVADOS CREAM

Fallen apples, damp earth and the intense cidery smell of last year's apples stored in the dusty hay loft. Such memories are the making of recipes.

**SERVES 6**

**For the pancake batter:**

**55 g plain flour**

**60 g buckwheat flour**

**pinch of salt**

**1 medium egg, beaten**

**200 ml milk**

**1 tablespoon melted butter**

**sunflower oil for frying**

**For the apple filling and cream:**

**6 medium Cox's Orange Pippins**

**1 tablespoon lemon juice**

**55 g butter, plus extra for baking**

**55 g sultanas**

**30 g caster sugar**

**3½ tablespoons Calvados**

**200 ml double cream**

**1 tablespoon sifted icing sugar**

Sift the flours and salt into a bowl and make a well in the centre. Using a wooden spoon, slowly mix the egg into the flour until it starts to form a smooth paste. Beat in the milk, bit by bit, followed by 85 ml water and the butter until you have a smooth batter. Strain into a jug and leave to rest for 30 minutes.

Set a small (15 cm) heavy frying pan over a medium-high heat. Lightly oil and, when the pan is very hot, pour in about 2 tablespoons of batter. Rotate the pan so that it is evenly coated in a thin layer. Once the batter begins to set and form small bubbles, loosen the edges with a greased palette knife and flip over. Cook for another minute, then slip the pancake on to a plate. Grease the pan once more and repeat. As you cook, you will need to reduce the heat slightly. This should make about 12 pancakes. Cover and set aside.

Peel, quarter, core and thickly slice the apples into a large bowl. Toss with the lemon juice. Set a large frying pan over a medium heat. Melt the butter and stir in the apples and sultanas. Fry for about 3 minutes, stirring regularly, until the apples are golden and just tender, then reduce the heat and mix in the sugar and 2 tablespoons Calvados. Continue to cook for 4 minutes or until the apples are soft and juicy. Tip into a bowl.

Whisk together the cream and 1½ tablespoons Calvados until the cream forms soft peaks. Cover and chill.

Preheat the oven to Gas Mark 4/180°C. Liberally butter an ovenproof gratin dish. Take the first pancake and spoon some of the cooked apple over half of the pancake. Fold the pancake over so that the apple mixture is covered, then fold the pancake in half again so that it forms a quarter. Place in the gratin dish. Once all the pancakes are filled, lightly dot with butter and cover the dish with foil. Bake for 20 minutes or until piping hot. Serve dusted with icing sugar and with lots of Calvados cream.

# **APRIL** VERDANT

## THE LUSH GREEN SCENT
## OF FRESHLY MOWN GRASS

Certain flavours capture the pure essence of a season.
Spring, for example, is the smell of wood sorrel, ground elder
and wild garlic bruised underfoot in frowsy green woodland.
It is the scent of rain falling on lush vegetation and the flavour
of crushed watercress and chopped parsley, and with it comes
a feeling of bubbling optimism. Few cooks can resist the lure
of cooking with verdant flavours.

   I, for one, start to seek out an array of edible green
shoots, herbs and leaves as soon as I smell spring in the city
air. Suddenly, pea shoots, red-stemmed chard and even
punnets of wheat grass look alluring. Their fragile beauty

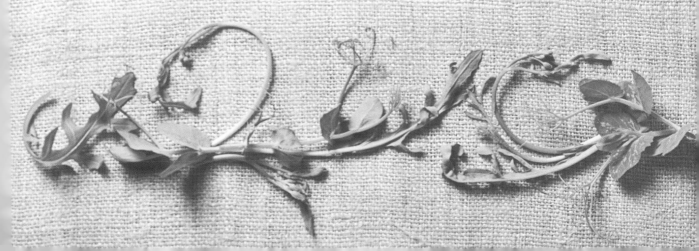

invites creativity. How to provoke in the eater that illusive *joie de vie* that comes with spring?

Chefs tend to intensify verdant aromas by distilling green leaves into vivid-tasting purées and dressings. However, smooth textures can make verdant flavours taste slightly one dimensional and flat, which somehow seems at odds with the dappled nature of spring. Add greater texture and you will release myriad verdant notes. Bite into a leafy salad that contains sprigs of watercress, sorrel and tarragon and you will experience an explosion of sappy flavours as you eat.

Many verdant flavours are quite ephemeral. The green notes of herbs and leaves quickly fade when subjected to heat, so they should always be added at the last moment or used raw. Mix chopped parsley into a creamy fish soup just before serving and it will taste amazing, but add it too early and the parsley turns dull. There are exceptions to this rule, such as peas or spinach – both of which will retain their fresh verdant flavour if blanched. The Japanese have refined this art perfectly, so that many verdant-flavoured ingredients such as watercress or cabbage leaves are submerged for a few seconds in boiling water before being refreshed under cold water and squeezed dry. The blanched green is then reheated at the last moment in a hot broth or stew. As it happens, blanching also lessens the bitterness of such leaves, which ensures that we are more aware of their subtle verdant flavour.

It helps to sniff the spring air before trying to create a verdant-flavoured dish that evokes that delicious feeling of optimism. The smell of wallflowers and fresh cut grass in an urban park suggests combining floral and citrus flavours with verdant notes, such as you might taste in a sweet-sour lemon balm dip for a prawn wonton. A spring meadow evokes the herbal and creamy tones that you might find in a herb cream cheese and watercress sandwich.

Yet, try as I might, I have not yet succeeded in creating a verdant-flavoured pudding. Verdant flavours tend to have bitter undertones that are too strongly associated with savoury dishes. Hence, no sweet morsel to end this chapter.

## LETTUCE, WATERCRESS AND PEA SOUP

Depth is added to this creamy soup by combining several different verdant-flavoured foods. These are then released together in the mouth to create layers of fresh green flavour.

**SERVES 4**

**4 tablespoons extra virgin olive oil**

**1 large onion, diced**

**2 inner sticks celery, diced**

**1 clove garlic, diced**

**750 ml chicken stock**

**170 g frozen petit pois**

**150 g cos lettuce leaves**

**1 bunch watercress**

**150 ml double cream**

**salt and freshly ground black pepper**

**½ small bunch chives, finely snipped**

Set a large saucepan over a low heat and, once hot, add the oil followed by the onion, celery and garlic. Fry gently for 10 minutes or until the vegetables are soft and golden. Add the stock, increase the heat, bring up to the boil and add the peas. Return to the boil, then reduce to a simmer, cover and cook for 10 minutes.

Meanwhile, wash and finely slice the lettuce leaves. Wash the watercress, strip the leaves from the stems and roughly slice the watercress leaves. Discard the stems. Add the lettuce and watercress to the peas after they've simmered for 10 minutes, then continue to simmer for a further 10 minutes.

Purée the soup, stir in 100 ml cream and season to taste. Reheat to piping hot, divide between four bowls and swirl in the remaining cream. Add a few snipped chives and serve.

## LEEK, TARRAGON AND QUAIL'S EGG SALAD

The best Japanese chefs have perfected the art of using colour, texture, taste and flavour in each dish to capture the mood of a season. This concept can be transposed into a Western context. Here, spring is suggested on a number of levels by the young leeks, eggs and an airy arrangement of verdant-flavoured leaves and herbs.

**SERVES 4**

**12 quail's eggs**

**20 baby leeks (about 525 g)**

**1 teaspoon smooth Dijon mustard**

**2 tablespoons white wine vinegar**

**6 tablespoons extra virgin olive oil**

**1 tablespoon tarragon leaves, snipped**

**salt and freshly ground black pepper**

**100 g mixed rocket and red chard leaves**

Place the eggs in a small saucepan. Cover with cold water and bring up to the boil. Cook for 2 minutes then remove and cool under cold running water before peeling.

Trim the leeks, cut away their roots and darkest part of their leaves. Remove their tough outer leaves and cut a cross in the pale green sections – to create a mop-like effect. Wash them thoroughly in a sinkful of cold water.

Bring a large pan of water to the boil and add the leeks. Return to the boil and cook briskly for 3 minutes or until the leeks are just tender. Drain and cool under cold running water, then pat dry on kitchen paper.

In a large bowl, whisk together the mustard, vinegar and olive oil. Add the tarragon and seasoning to taste. Set aside until needed.

When you are ready to serve, mix the leeks into the vinaigrette, followed by the salad leaves. Divide into airy piles between four plates. Halve the eggs and tuck six egg halves into each salad. Serve immediately.

## SPICED CRAB SALAD

Different emotional associations can be drawn upon in a verdant recipe by including other flavours. Here, a sense of freedom and escapism is added by including fresh citrus and ozone-flavoured crab.

**SERVES 4**

**300 g white crab meat**

**2 organic limes**

**1 small red Thai chilli (or to taste), finely chopped**

**salt and freshly ground black pepper**

**4 Little Gem lettuce hearts**

**1 bunch watercress, trimmed and washed**

**1 tablespoon roughly sliced mint leaves**

**a handful coriander leaves**

**4 trimmed spring onions, finely sliced**

**5 inner sticks celery, finely sliced**

**1 red pepper, quartered, deseeded and finely sliced**

**4 tablespoons extra virgin olive oil**

Pick through the crab meat and remove any tiny pieces of shell. Gently squeeze out any excess moisture and place the meat in a bowl. Finely grate and juice 1 lime. Mix the zest and juice into the crab meat. Add the chilli and season to taste.

Wash the lettuce leaves and pat dry. Place the smaller leaves in a mixing bowl with the watercress sprigs, mint, coriander, spring onions, celery and red pepper.

When you are ready to serve, toss the watercress salad in 2 tablespoons of lime juice from the second lime and the extra virgin olive oil. Season to taste and divide between four plates. Spoon the crab meat on to eight remaining larger lettuce leaves and place two on each plate. Serve immediately.

# SPINACH RISOTTO

Blanching green vegetables such as spinach and watercress helps to capture their verdant flavour. In this recipe, I play on the contrast between the creamy texture of the risotto and the fresh spring flavour of the spinach and herbs.

**SERVES 4 AS A MAIN COURSE**

**1 litre good chicken stock (see page 168)**

**a pinch of saffron threads**

**salt**

**2 tablespoons extra virgin olive oil**

**55 g unsalted butter**

**2 onions, finely diced**

**300 g Arborio or Vialone Nano rice**

**200 ml dry white wine, such as Muscadet**

**800 g washed baby leaf spinach**

**1 small bunch chives or a few wild garlic leaves, finely snipped**

**1 tablespoon finely sliced basil**

**30 g finely grated Parmesan, plus extra for serving**

**freshly ground black pepper**

Heat the stock to simmering point in a saucepan. Place the saffron threads in a small bowl, add a tiny pinch of salt and roughly crush under a teaspoon. Mix into the hot stock.

Put the oil and butter in a wide heavy-bottomed saucepan. Set over a low heat. Gently fry the onions for 10 minutes or until soft. Add the rice and stir for 2 minutes until it looks translucent,.

Mix in the wine, allow to bubble up and, when it has almost evaporated, stir in a ladleful of hot stock. Simmer briskly, stirring regularly. Once the stock has been absorbed, add another ladleful of hot stock. Keep repeating the process. After about 18–20 minutes the stock should be used up and the rice should be tender and cooked in a sloppy sauce.

Meanwhile, blanch the spinach by dropping half of it into a large pan of boiling water. As soon as it wilts, drain and cool with cold running water. Repeat the process with the remaining spinach. Squeeze dry and roughly chop.

Remove the risotto from the heat. Stir the spinach and sliced herbs into the rice. Add the cheese and season to taste. Once the spinach has heated through, serve with extra Parmesan.

## STIR FRIED PEA SHOOTS

Pea shoots are usually cut from newly sprouted peas and have an intense verdant flavour of fresh peas. A taste of spring.

If feeling especially healthy, you can cook freshly sprouted shoots with their sprouted seed attached, as shown in the photograph. They add a slightly nutty flavour to a verdant dish.

**SERVES 2**

**1 tablespoon sunflower oil**

**2 fine slices peeled ginger**

**1 clove garlic, finely chopped**

**200 g pea shoots**

**salt**

Set a non-stick frying pan or wok over a high heat. Add the oil, then the ginger slices to the oil. As soon as the ginger begins to colour, remove from the oil and discard and add the garlic. Let the garlic sizzle for a few seconds then mix in the pea shoots. Add a pinch of salt and stir fry briskly for a few seconds. Serve as soon as the pea shoots collapse and turn bright green.

# GRILLED LOBSTER WITH SORREL SAUCE

This sour verdant sauce tastes wonderful with all manner of seafood.

**SERVES 4**
**2 x 750–800 g or 4 x 500 g live lobsters**
**½ bunch spring onions, finely sliced**
**140 ml double cream**
**1 small bunch or 3 supermarket packets sorrel**
**salt and freshly ground black pepper**
**15 g butter, melted**

To kill the lobsters painlessly, place them in the freezer. The time varies according to the size, but a 500 g lobster needs about 1–1½ hours, while an 800 g lobster needs nearer 2 hours. You don't want their flesh to freeze.

Prepare the sauce. Place the spring onions in a small pan with the cream and set over a low heat. Bring slowly to the boil, then simmer for 5 minutes. Wash the sorrel, discard any tough stems and cut the leaves into fine strips. Mix two-thirds of the sorrel into the hot cream. Simmer until the sorrel wilts, then remove from the heat and liquidise. Add the remaining sorrel and purée briefly. Return to the pan and season to taste. Set aside until needed.

Preheat the grill to medium high. Remove the lobsters from the freezer. Place the first lobster belly-side down on a chopping board. Cut in half lengthways, starting at the cross on their back and down through their head before cutting down the length of their body. Remove the stomach sac; this will have been cut in half but looks like a slightly clear pouch in the head section. Remove the intestinal tract from the tail section. Repeat with the remaining lobsters. Remove the elastic bands from their claws.

Arrange the lobster halves on a baking tray, cut side up, and brush the meat with the melted butter. Set under the grill for 10 minutes or until cooked through. Reheat the sauce and serve with the lobsters.

# RABBIT WITH WATERCRESS

Verdant notes, such as watercress, introduce the illusion of lightness to rich dishes. Rabbit tastes like chicken, but most people find the shape of the joints off-putting, so a sensible cook will woo them by boning the saddles to remove the loin. This is much easier than you might think provided you have a sharp knife. Some supermarkets sell what are termed 'rabbit cutlets'. These are chopped saddles and can be boned as described below.

**SERVES 4**

**1.4 kg skinned rabbit cutlets (saddles)**

**1 tablespoon olive oil**

**30 g unsalted butter**

**salt and freshly ground black pepper**

**425 ml good chicken stock (see page 168)**

**140 ml crème fraîche**

**2 leeks, white parts only, finely sliced**

**1 carrot, peeled and finely sliced**

**1 inner stick celery, finely sliced**

**8 button mushrooms, finely sliced**

**4 tablespoons finely chopped watercress leaves**

Place the first saddle in front of you fleshy side up. Run your finger over the flesh, feeling where the bones are, then, using the point of your knife, cut along the length of the backbone, keeping as close to the bone as possible. Work your way down underneath the plump fillet and back out the other side. The fillet will fall away. Repeat the process with the fillet on the other side of the backbone. Discard the bones and thin flaps of meat and cut the loin into 2.5-cm chunks. Chill the meat until needed.

Set a wide saucepan over a medium heat. Add the oil and 15 g butter. Season the diced fillets. Add half to the hot fat and fry briskly for a minute or until golden. Remove and fry the remaining meat. Discard the fat from the pan. Add the chicken stock and crème fraîche. Bring up to the boil, simmer for 5 minutes, then add the leeks, carrot and celery. Simmer briskly for 10 minutes.

Melt the remaining 15 g butter in a small frying pan. Add the sliced mushrooms and fry briskly for 2 minutes, then mix into the vegetables with the rabbit. Simmer gently for a further 5 minutes then add the watercress and season to taste. Leave to rest for 10 minutes to allow the liquid to reabsorb into the meat, then serve with rice.

# MAY CREAM

## BUTTER MELTING IN YOUR MOUTH

The subtle scent of cream instantly evokes the luscious texture of fat-rich foods such as butter, yoghurt and soft-cooked eggs. For me, this blend of flavour and texture induces a dreamy sense of detachment. Creamy ingredients conjure up a cool world of stone-floored kitchens, china bowls and buttercup meadows. Life instantly quietens as one bites into a thickly buttered slice of fresh bread or slowly licks a vanilla ice cream. Cream-flavoured foods are definitely conducive to thought.

The pleasure that most of us associate with eating creamy foods is partly due to the fact that we have receptors in the brain that not only register individual flavours and tastes, but also different textures in food, including 'fat textured' food. Professor Edmund Rolls writes in his book, *Emotion Explained* (2005), that 'texture

in the mouth is also an important indicator of whether fat is present in the food, which is important not only as a high value energy source, but also as a potential source of essential fatty acids.' In other words, it seems that we have evolved to favour such textures, in much the same way as we have developed a taste for sweetness because it indicates a good source of energy.

Since creamy textures are enjoyed by most eaters, it is worth exploiting them in relation to dairy flavours. However, a little bit of creamy lusciousness goes a long way, so it is important to partner it with contrasting tastes, flavours and textures. Whipped cream, for example, seems cloying eaten on its own but becomes light and fragrant when munched on a crisp-shelled meringue. Add a few tart raspberries and it becomes utterly irresistible. Similarly, eggs baked with cream 'en cocotte' need crisp toast to offset their unctuous texture. Add a little umami-tasting ham or a pinch of peppery flavoured tarragon leaves and they will seem twice as appetising.

It helps to step back slightly when trying to create cream-flavoured dishes, particularly as creamy notes work well with most categories of flavour. What mood are you trying to instil in the eater? What references are you drawing upon? Soft herbal, floral and verdant notes, for example, will suggest spring and summer. Thick slices of mozzarella, strewn with basil and splashed with olive oil instantly evoke the heat of eating al fresco in Italy. Smoky, caramel or spice notes are more likely to hint at autumn or winter. Imagine a scoop of toffee ice cream melting into a slice of warm apple pie and you can almost smell the windfalls and wood smoke. In either case, the eater slips into their own world and concentrates on the sheer pleasure of creamy notes filling their mouth. Silence falls.

## CREAMY SCRAMBLED EGGS WITH CHIVES

There was a time when cooks would distinguish between 'buttered' and 'scrambled' eggs. According to Constance Spry and Rosemary Hume in *The Constance Spry Cookery Book* (1956), the former is more cloying and rich as it is made without any cream or milk to lighten it. They might have added that cream also imbues the eggs with a delicious flavour.

**SERVES 2**

**3 medium eggs, beaten**
**2 tablespoons single cream**
**salt and freshly ground black pepper**
**15 g unsalted butter**
**1 tablespoon finely chopped chives**
**2 slices buttered toast**

In a bowl, beat together the eggs, cream and a little salt and freshly ground black pepper with a fork. Melt the butter in a small non-stick pan over a low heat. Pour in the egg mixture, stirring with a wooden spoon until the eggs are scrambled, but loosely set. Remove the pan from the heat, add the chives and continue to stir until the eggs are cooked to your liking.

Place a slice of lightly buttered toast on each plate and spoon the scrambled egg on top. Serve immediately.

## BUTTERED PRAWNS

You need a good quality unsalted French butter for this recipe to ensure that the dish is imbued with delicate, slightly sour, buttery notes that perfectly offset the buttery textured prawns.

**SERVES 2**

**55 g unsalted French butter**
**a pinch of cayenne pepper**
**200 g peeled, cooked North Atlantic prawns**
**1 tablespoon lemon juice**
**freshly ground black pepper**

Put the butter and cayenne pepper in a small pan and set over a low heat. Remove as soon as the butter has melted.

Meticulously dry the prawns by squeezing out the excess water and patting dry with lots of kitchen paper. Roughly chop them and place in a mixing bowl. Stir in the melted butter and season to taste with the lemon juice and black pepper. Tightly pack into 2 x 100 ml soufflé pots and chill until needed.

Serve with lots of hot buttered toast for an indulgent lunch, preferably with a few cornichons to nibble.

## GREEN SALAD WITH ELIZA ACTON'S ENGLISH SAUCE

Soft herbal notes in cream hint at summer, making it work surprisingly well with verdant-flavoured foods such as salad leaves, cucumber and tarragon. I've adapted this elegant Eliza Acton recipe to illustrate the point. Try serving this salad with hot roast chicken or cold roast beef.

**SERVES 6**

**For the dressing:**

1 medium egg, at room temperature

salt and freshly ground black pepper

a pinch of cayenne pepper

70 ml double cream

1 tablespoon tarragon vinegar

1 teaspoon roughly sliced tarragon

**For the salad:**

4 plump, soft round lettuces

½ cucumber, peeled and finely sliced

1½ small bunches chives, snipped

3 handfuls mixed baby red chard and spinach leaves

Place the egg in a pan, cover with cold water and bring up to a gentle boil. Simmer for 8 minutes or until hard boiled. Drain, cool and peel. Discard the egg white and sieve the egg yolk into a small bowl or thoroughly mash with a fork. Season with salt, black pepper and cayenne pepper. Beat in 1 teaspoon of cold water followed by the cream, vinegar and fresh tarragon. The result should be a delicately flavoured cream.

Twist out the hearts of your lettuces – the outer leaves can be used for Lettuce, watercress and pea soup (see page 51). Separate the inner leaves before washing and drying. Place in a mixing bowl with the cucumber, chives, red chard and spinach leaves. When you are ready, lightly mix the cream into the salad and serve immediately.

## ASPARAGUS WITH BEURRE BLANC

The ultimate in butter sauces, this classic recipe is very easy to make. Its wonderful texture will ensure that your guests melt with pleasure even before they start to detect its delicious buttery notes.

**SERVES 4**

**24 stems medium asparagus**

**salt**

**3 tablespoons Muscadet wine**

**3 tablespoons white wine vinegar**

**3 shallots, very finely chopped**

**freshly ground black pepper (optional)**

**170 g good quality, cold, French unsalted butter, roughly diced**

Warm four plates in a cool oven. Prepare the asparagus. Wash thoroughly in plenty of cold water to loosen any sand from the tips, trim the stems, cut off any woody inedible parts and, if necessary, use a potato peeler to pare the lower part of the stems. Drop into a large pan of salted boiling water and cook for 8 minutes or until the stems are tender but still retain a little bite. Drain and spread out on a plate lined with kitchen paper. Pat dry and keep warm.

Meanwhile, place the wine, vinegar and chopped shallots in a small non-corrosive saucepan. Set over a low heat and boil until the shallots are soft and the wine and vinegar have reduced to a hint of liquid beneath the shallots. Remove from the heat and lightly season.

Once everything is ready, reheat the shallot mixture over a low heat. Once hot, whisk in a few small pieces of butter. As you whisk, the butter will form an emulsion with the warm vinegar. Keep whisking, adding a few more pieces of butter as it emulsifies, until all the butter is used and the sauce has thickened into a pale warm sauce the same consistency as runny double cream. Do not let the mixture boil at any stage or it will split. Adjust the seasoning to taste.

Divide the asparagus between the four warm plates. Pour the beurre blanc over the tips of the asparagus and serve immediately.

## CREAMY CHICKEN PIE

Once you become sensitised to creamy flavours, you can start to play with them. Here, the light buttery notes in the pastry resonate with the richer tones of the clotted cream in the sauce, filling your mouth with luscious textures.

If feeling extravagant, you can mix a handful of fresh morels in with the button mushrooms. To prepare them, trim their stems and rinse thoroughly before cutting in half lengthways. Set aside with the button mushrooms.

**SERVES 4**

**225 g shortcrust pastry (see page 169)**
**4 plump chicken breasts, skinned**
**5–6 tablespoons sunflower oil**
**4 tablespoons plain flour**
**salt and freshly ground black pepper**
**1 onion, finely diced**
**1 clove garlic, finely chopped**
**4 medium carrots, peeled and sliced**
**150 g button mushrooms, halved**
**200 ml dry white wine**
**500 ml good chicken stock**
   **(see page 168)**
**2 strips finely pared lemon zest**
**100 ml clotted or double cream**
**½ egg, beaten**

Roll out the pastry to fit the top of a pie dish or a 1 litre pudding basin. Chill in the fridge. Line the edge of your dish with a strip of pastry. Set aside.

Preheat the oven to Gas Mark 6/200°C. Cut the chicken breasts into small chunks. Set a large non-stick frying pan over a medium-high heat. Add 3 tablespoons oil. Dust the chicken in 2 tablespoons seasoned flour and fry in batches, adding another tablespoon of oil if necessary. As soon as the meat is sealed and flecked gold, transfer to the pie dish.

Add 2 more tablespoons oil to the frying pan and reduce the heat to low. Add the onion and garlic and fry for 3 minutes before adding the carrots. Continue to fry for 3 further minutes or until the onion is soft and golden, then mix in the mushrooms. Fry for 3 minutes, then stir in the remaining 2 tablespoons plain flour and cook for a minute, stirring occasionally. Stir in the wine and boil vigorously until reduced by two thirds, then add the stock and lemon zest. Boil until reduced by half. Add the cream and boil until it has thickened slightly. Season to taste and mix into the chicken in the pie dish.

Lightly brush the pastry rim with some beaten egg. Cover with the pastry lid. Seal the edges with a fork or by crimping the pastry with your fingers. Brush the lid with some beaten egg, prick with a small knife and bake in the preheated oven for 35–40 minutes or until the pastry is crisp and golden.

## SEARED SALMON WITH CUCUMBER BUTTERMILK

Modern buttermilk is cultured and has a refreshing, slightly sour taste that cuts through the natural richness of the salmon. Its light summery dairy flavour is amplified by adding herbal or verdant flavours, such as here with the chives and cucumber.

**SERVES 4**

**200 ml buttermilk**

**½ cucumber, peeled**

**⅔ small bunch chives, finely snipped**

**salt and freshly ground black pepper**

**4 x 150 g portions organic salmon fillet**

**1½ tablespoons extra virgin olive oil**

Preheat an oven-top griddle pan over a medium-high heat. Pour the buttermilk into a small bowl. Roughly grate the cucumber and squeeze out the excess liquid before mixing into the buttermilk. Add the chives and season to taste.

Lightly coat the salmon fillets with the olive oil and season with salt and freshly ground black pepper. Place the fish, flesh-side down, in the pan and cook for 4–6 minutes before turning over and cooking for another 4–6 minutes or until the fish is just cooked through. The time will vary according to the thickness of your fillets. Serve with the cucumber buttermilk.

## POACHED APRICOTS WITH YOGHURT SORBET

Creamy flavours work perfectly in frozen puddings as their flavour is gently released in the mouth as they melt into a delicious fat-rich liquid. This recipe can be adapted to loquats, which are sold in May. Loquats actually grow in the south of England, but tend not to ripen here until the end of June.

**SERVES 4**
**300 g granulated sugar**
**1 vanilla pod, split**
**500 g natural Greek yoghurt**
**500 g apricots or loquats**

Put the sugar, vanilla pod and 150 ml water in a small heavy-based saucepan. Set over a low heat and stir occasionally until the sugar has dissolved. Bring up to the boil and simmer for 10 minutes.

Remove the vanilla pod and keep to one side. Measure the liquid and pour one third into a wide non-corrosive saucepan.

Slowly whisk the remaining two thirds of the liquid into the yoghurt. Scrape the excess vanilla seeds from the inside of the pod into the mixture. Pour the yoghurt mixture into your ice cream machine and churn according to the manufacturer's instructions. Alternatively, pour into a shallow container and, after the first hour, mix with a fork every 40 minutes or so to ensure it has an even texture.

Meanwhile, halve and stone the apricots. If using loquats, halve, stone and peel the fruit. Arrange in a single layer in the saucepan with the syrup. Add the vanilla pod, cover and set over a low heat. Cook the apricots very gently for 5–6 minutes (or 2–3 minutes if using loquats) until they are barely tender. Remove from the heat and leave to cool in the syrup. They will continue to cook as they cool. Transfer to a bowl, cover and chill until needed.

Serve the sorbet with the cold poached fruit and its delicious juices.

## CRÉMETS WITH STRAWBERRIES

As Elizabeth David wrote in *French Provincial Cooking* (1960), 'In its [les crémets'] extreme simplicity this sweet, native to Anjou and Saumur, is one of the most delicious in all French Cookery.' The lightly soured, creamy flavour conjures up early summer, especially when eaten in May with fragrant Gariguette strawberries. The French serve crémets covered in cream!

**SERVES 6**

**170 g full fat crème fraîche**

**170 g full fat fromage frais**

**3 medium egg whites**

**450 g strawberries, hulled and sliced**

**caster sugar to taste**

Crémets need to be able to drain off their excess liquid naturally, so you will need six muslin-lined perforated crémet moulds. You can buy perforated china heart-shaped moulds. Otherwise, the French recommend boring your own holes into individual yoghurt pots – although I have not tried this. Line each mould with a small square of clean muslin that you've rinsed and wrung dry. Set aside.

Whisk the crème fraîche in a large mixing bowl until it holds soft peaks. Whisk the fromage frais in a separate bowl to remove any tiny lumps, then fold into the crème fraîche. Finally, whisk the egg whites in a clean bowl until they form stiff peaks, then gently fold into the crème fraîche mixture.

Spoon into the prepared moulds. Fold the muslin up around the top of each crémet. Set a cooling rack over a shallow baking tray in the fridge. This will allow the crémets to drip freely as they firm up. Arrange the crémet moulds on the rack and chill for a minimum of 6 hours, but preferably for nearer 12 hours.

To serve, unfold the muslin on top of each crémet, turn each one out of its mould, delicately unwrap and place each crémet on its own pudding plate. Toss the strawberries in the sugar. Spoon on to each plate and sprinkle the hearts with caster sugar.

**JUNE** FLORAL

## HONEYSUCKLE ON A WARM SUMMER'S EVENING

Playing with floral notes in food is like adding delicate flecks of white to a dark painting. They add lightness to a dish, creating the illusion of eating outside amidst flowery summer scents and the hum of insects. There is a soft sweetness about them that it is impossible for a daydreaming cook to resist. The fresh scent of lavender, for example, brings out the exquisite notes of pear in a lavender-pear ice cream, just as the mere suggestion of orange flower water enhances the sweet flavours of raw carrots in a lemon-dressed Moroccan salad.

As with all odours, memories and their associated emotions will colour how you use floral flavours in your cooking. For many rural British cooks there is something magical about the drowsy smell of sun-baked roses and pinks on a midsummer's afternoon, or the heady fragrance of elderflowers after a sudden shower of rain. For an urban cook, such as myself, who grew up in the country, a splash of rosewater in a lemon cup cake or a sprig of elderflower infused into a gooseberry fool will instantly conjure up a child-like sense of escapism and unreality. Over time, memories and culinary ideas intermingle – rambling roses mix with tales from *The Arabian Nights* in rhubarb and rosewater jelly; damp elderflowers and stinging nettles evoke pickled elderflower gooseberries.

The subtle yet complex nuances of floral scents can be found in many foods, ranging from a good honey to a soft young goat's cheese. Combine these with other summer flavours such as verdant, creamy, herbal or fruit aromas, and you will create intensely evocative dishes that resonate with the smell of summer. Goat's cheese tossed in warm pasta with thyme flowers, lemon zest and chopped fresh herbs, for example, conjures up for me the wild, sharp fragrance of the North Downs on a hot June day.

A cool kitchen is the perfect place to experiment with such delicious flavours. Consider the undertones in your floral-flavoured food. Lavender, for example, has citrus, peppery and herbal notes within its scent that work well with savoury ingredients such as lime gravad lax or roast lamb with rocket salad. Always use floral scents moderately. The aromatic, heady notes of a Muscat wine, for instance, can intensify the sweet fragrance of seared meat, but too much will imbue the meat with an unpleasant cloying flavour. It is a matter of becoming aware of the myriad different floral scents around you and capturing them in your food.

# WILD LEAF, PEAR AND GOAT'S CHEESE SALAD

In the seventeenth century, aromatic gillyflowers (pinks), violets, primroses and cowslips were pickled in sugar and vinegar and routinely added to salads. Modern palates prefer the more delicate flavours of a few fresh petals or of vinegar infused with flowers to add an unexpected light note to a dish.

This recipe makes more lavender vinegar than you will need. Keep it and use it for other salads. The excess can be stored in a sterilised jar for up to a year. It should be made at least 2 hours before needed but is best made a day ahead.

**SERVES 6**

**150 ml white wine vinegar**

**5 sprigs lavender flowers, washed**

**6 ripe pears**

**1½ tablespoons lemon juice**

**6 x 60 g fresh goat's cheeses, such as Innes Button**

**4½ tablespoons extra virgin olive oil, plus extra for drizzling**

**salt and freshly ground black pepper**

**150 g mixed wild rocket and red chard**

Place the vinegar in a non-corrosive saucepan. Bring to the boil, remove from the heat, add the lavender and cover. Leave to infuse for at least 2 hours.

Preheat the grill to medium high. Core and quarter the pears – there is no need to peel them. Finely slice each quarter lengthways and mix with the lemon juice in a large bowl.

Place the cheeses on an oiled baking sheet and drizzle each with a little olive oil. Grill for 3-4 minutes, or until they are beginning to melt and are slightly golden.

Meanwhile, whisk together 1½ tablespoons lavender vinegar with 4½ tablespoons extra virgin olive oil. Season to taste. Add the salad leaves to the sliced pear, mix in the vinaigrette and arrange in airy piles on six plates. Slip a hot cheese to one side of each salad, scatter a few vinegary lavender flowers on to the salad and serve immediately.

## ELDERFLOWER VINEGAR

One of the pleasures of cooking is to capture the scent of a moment. This can then be used later in the year to surprise the eater. In 1787 Mrs Raffald, in her wonderful book *The Experienced English House-keeper*, advises that elderflower vinegar should be made with equal volumes of elderflowers and vinegar. 'It makes a pretty mixture on a side-table, with tarragon vinegar, lemon pickle, &c.', she says.

This recipe can be adapted to other edible fragrant flowers such as lavender, pinks (*Dianthus*) and meadowsweet (*Filipendula ulmaria*), all of which will add a summery light flavour to a winter salad.

**MAKES 300 ML VINEGAR**
**5 large elderflower heads**
**300 ml good quality white wine vinegar**

Sterilise a 500 g jam jar with a non-metal lid (vinegar will corrode metal lids over time) in the dishwasher and leave to steam dry.

Dip the elderflowers in a bowl of cool water to remove any wildlife or dust. Leave to dry on kitchen paper. Once dry, strip enough tiny white flowers from their green stems to nearly fill the sterilised jar.

Add the vinegar, allowing an air space at the top of approximately 1.5 cm. Seal and place on a sunny windowsill for 2 weeks or until it tastes good. Strain through muslin and decant into a sterilised bottle or jar. Seal, label and store in a cool dark place.

# GRILLED MACKEREL WITH GOOSEBERRY ELDERFLOWER RELISH

Gooseberries and elderflowers briefly overlap in June. This Japanese method of salting oily fish removes some of the fishy odours and firms up its texture. The fragrant, sweet-sour gooseberries will enhance the mackerel's natural sweetness and lift its flavour. You can also cook the mackerel over a hot barbecue. If you can't find any fresh elderflowers, use 1 tablespoon of good quality elderflower cordial instead.

**SERVES 4**

**1 elderflower head**

**85 g granulated sugar**

**2 strips finely pared lemon zest**

**1 tablespoon white wine vinegar**

**340 g gooseberries, topped and tailed**

**4 medium-sized mackerel, filleted**

**2 teaspoons fine sea salt**

**2 tablespoons extra virgin olive oil**

**1 lemon, quartered**

Dip the elderflower head in a bowl of cool water to remove any wildlife or dust. Place the sugar, elderflower, lemon zest, vinegar and 100 ml water into a non-corrosive pan and dissolve the sugar over a low heat. Simmer gently for 5 minutes before adding the gooseberries. Cover and simmer gently for 6 minutes or until they are soft but still holding their shape. Using a slotted spoon, remove the gooseberries to a clean bowl, leaving the flowers in the syrup. Boil this liquid until it is thick and syrupy, then mix into the gooseberries and leave to cool. If you don't have any elderflowers, add 1 tablespoon elderflower cordial at this stage.

Gently rinse the fish fillets under cold water and pat dry on kitchen paper. Cut the skin of each fillet diagonally three times and lightly and evenly sprinkle with fine sea salt on both sides. Cover and chill for 30 minutes.

Preheat two griddle pans over a medium heat or light a barbecue. Rinse the fish under the cold tap. Pat dry on kitchen paper and lightly oil. Cook flesh side down for 3 minutes before flipping over and cooking for a further 3 minutes. Remove the elderflower and lemon zest from the tepid gooseberry relish. Serve the fish immediately with the lemon wedges and gooseberry relish.

## LINDEN BLOSSOM HONEY ROAST DUCK

Honey can be a useful way of adding the lightest of light floral flavour. Artisan honeys contain many floral fragrances depending on where the bees have foraged. Apple blossom honey, for example, tastes different from linden blossom or heather honey. Mass-produced honey has a duller, more uniform flavour as it is usually blended from different honeys and then flash heated, which destroys many of its subtle floral characteristics.

To evoke a sultry June day, serve this fragrant duck with the Cannellini and broad beans with lavender on page 78 or with lush green spinach flavoured with a hint of mint and crème fraîche. Alternatively, toss the sliced duck with lightly dressed salad leaves, watercress, tarragon and mint. Add a generous handful of crisps and serve immediately.

**SERVES 6**
**3 tablespoons linden blossom or other artisan honey**
**finely grated zest and juice of 2 large limes**
**6 x 200 g duck breasts, skin on**
**salt and freshly ground black pepper**

Preheat the oven to Gas Mark 8/225°C. Melt the honey in a small non-corrosive saucepan over a very low heat. Remove from the heat and mix in the finely grated lime zest and juice.

Score diamonds into the skin of the duck breasts and season with salt and pepper. Set a dry non-stick frying pan over a medium-high heat. Once hot, place three of the duck breasts into the pan skin-side down. As soon as their fat turns golden brown – about 2 minutes – transfer them to a large bowl. Pour the duck fat from the pan into a small bowl. Repeat the process with the remaining three duck breasts. Pour the warm lime marinade over the duck. Coat thoroughly and leave to marinate for 10 minutes.

Heat 2 tablespoons of the duck fat in a non-stick roasting pan in the oven. Once sizzling hot, add the duck breasts, flesh side down and roast for 5 minutes. Baste with some of the marinade and continue to roast for a further 5 minutes. This will give you rosé duck breasts. Allow to rest in a warm place for 5 minutes before slicing thickly.

# RASPBERRY ROSEWATER ICE CREAM

There is a peculiar romance about adding distilled rose or orange flower water to puddings. The very act of letting a few fragrant drops splash into a strawberry or raspberry fool or an almond cream links you to a British culinary tradition that stretches back centuries. The modern kitchen momentarily fades into the seventeenth century stillroom, where gentlewomen added floral fragrances to the refined sweet concoctions they made for the delectation of their guests. Such aromas bring out the floral notes in raspberries and strawberries and add a breath of summer air to dairy flavours. The best quality distilled flower waters are found in Middle Eastern shops.

**SERVES 4**

**400 g raspberries**

**4 medium egg yolks**

**225 g caster sugar**

**285 ml double cream**

**2 teaspoons distilled rosewater**

**1 tablespoon kirsch**

Purée the raspberries and pass through a sieve into a large mixing bowl. Place the egg yolks and sugar in a separate mixing bowl. Whisk together until thick and pale.

Pour the cream into a saucepan and set over a medium heat. Bring up to the boil then remove from the heat and gradually whisk into the egg yolks and sugar. Return the mixture to the saucepan and set over a low heat, stirring continuously with a wooden spoon until it forms a thick custard. This will take about 20 minutes. Do not let it boil. If you think the custard is becoming too hot, remove the pan from the heat and keep stirring briskly. Once it has cooled slightly, return to the heat. You must not stop stirring or leave the custard unattended during this stage as it can easily split. The custard should be thick enough to hold a faint trail.

Strain the custard into the raspberry purée. Mix in the rosewater and kirsch. Remember that food tastes less sweet and less sour once it is frozen. Cover and chill until cold.

If you have an ice cream machine, churn the raspberry mixture according to the machine's instructions until it reaches a soft set. Transfer to a sealed container and store in the freezer until needed. If you do not have a machine, pour it into a shallow plastic container, cover and place in the fast-freeze compartment of your freezer. After the first hour, rework with a fork every 40 minutes until the mixture has frozen into a smooth, soft-set ice cream.

## CHAMOMILE JELLY WITH CHERRIES

When mentally searching for floral flavours, it is worth drawing on tisanes and teas for inspiration. The delicate citrus notes in a chamomile tisane, for example, are perfect for light-flavoured jellies, sorbets and fruit dressings. Add a touch of lemon with a hint of sweetness, and you will create a dreamy, ethereal pudding.

Those lucky enough to have highly scented German chamomile, *Chamaemelum nobile*, in their garden can use the fresh flowers in place of dried. This jelly is equally good served without the cherries, especially when accompanied by runny cream.

**SERVES 4**

**2 organic lemons**
**7 organic chamomile infusion tea bags**
**12 g sheet gelatine or 4 teaspoons (11.7 g sachet) powdered gelatine**
**170 g caster sugar**
**350 g cherries, halved and stoned**

Finely pare the lemon zest and divide equally between two small saucepans. Add 500 ml water to the first pan and 200 ml to the second. Bring both up to the boil and cook both briskly for 3 minutes. Remove both pans from the heat. Add 4 chamomile tea bags to the 500 ml water and 3 chamomile bags to the 200 ml. Leave both to infuse for 5 minutes. While infusing, soak the sheet gelatine in cold water for 5 minutes.

As soon as the 200 ml water has infused for 5 minutes, strain into a mixing bowl and mix in 55 g caster sugar. Stir until dissolved, then add 2 tablespoons lemon juice.

Drain off the water from the sheet gelatine, and pour the strained 500 ml hot chamomile water over the top. Squeeze out any excess liquid from the tea bags and add. Stir until the gelatine has dissolved. If using powdered gelatine, sprinkle the gelatine over about half of the 500 ml water. Leave to soak for 5 minutes then set over a low heat and stir occasionally until dissolved. Mix into the other half of the 500 ml water. Add the remaining 115 g caster sugar to the 500 ml chamomile water. Stir until it has dissolved, then add the juice from one lemon. Divide between four 150 ml jelly containers or pour into a pretty bowl. Cover and chill until set.

Add the cherries to the 200 ml sweetened chamomile water. Set aside until you're ready to serve the jelly. Serve with runny double cream to add a wonderful creamy summer note.

# **JULY** HERBAL

## ROSEMARY CRUSHED BETWEEN THE FINGERTIPS

Herbal flavours are amongst the easiest to identify in cooking – just think of the intense fragrance of basil scattered over a tomato salad or the unmistakable aroma of chicken roasted with rosemary. However, the easy familiarity of such herbs often leads to them being stereotyped, which in turn can limit their use. Rosemary and basil, for instance, are rarely used in sweet dishes, despite the fact that they can taste sublime combined with sugar. The art of the cook lies in recognising the potential of each herb and transposing it to new but equally delicious dishes. Thus lemon verbena, which is traditionally used in sweet dishes, brings out the delicate

flavour of pan-fried lamb, while basil adds a gorgeous peppery note to peaches simmered in  sugared wine.

At the height of summer, when all plant control is lost, the scent of herbs can hang heavy on the air. Brush past a patch of mint by the kitchen door and your clothes will become perfumed with peppermint. Throw down a rug on rolling dry pasture and your picnic may become scented by crushed wild marjoram. Even a sip of ginger beer will take on a wonderful aromatic flavour. Such experiences will shape how you cook. Perhaps the smell of salmon baking in the oven mixed with the smell of kitchen mint will inspire you to throw a few mint leaves into an accompanying green salad or make a fresh-tasting mint mayonnaise.

I have always found that the best way to develop interesting culinary ideas is to take small logical steps sideways. Thus, if the floral, woody aroma of vanilla tastes good infused in custard, so might a floral citrus flavour such as elderflower. And if that tastes good, which indeed it does, then the citrus peppery fragrance of basil or the peppery, herbal flavour of scented geraniums, *Pelargonium*, might also be intriguing. Such thoughts are often developed further through serendipitous reading. Elizabeth David in *Summer Cooking* (1955), for example, recommends in her recipe for Thick Blackberry Jelly, 'If possible, add 1 or 2 sweet-scented geranium leaves to the blackberries while they are stewing: these will give them a delicious flavour.' Suddenly the link between custard, blackberries and geranium leaves becomes stronger and all sorts of delectable permutations begin to suggest themselves.

## GREEN BEAN AND GRILLED PIGEON SALAD

Since lateral thinking is helpful when cooking with herbs, try marinating fish or meat after it has been lightly grilled or seared as this helps to capture the scent of freshly crushed herbs. The grilled pigeon breasts here are marinated in a summer herb, honey and walnut oil vinaigrette after they are cooked – perfect for a hot summer day.

**SERVES 4**

½ tablespoon honey

3 tablespoons white wine vinegar

9 tablespoons walnut oil

1 small shallot, finely chopped

½ small bunch parsley leaves, finely chopped

½ teaspoon finely chopped lemon thyme

½ tablespoon finely chopped mint

salt and freshly ground black pepper

6 wood pigeon breasts, skinned

1 tablespoon extra virgin olive oil

300 g green beans, trimmed

1 clove garlic, finely chopped

50 g walnut halves

100 g mixed baby salad leaves

Whisk the honey, 1 tablespoon vinegar and 3 tablespoons walnut oil together in a small bowl. Add the chopped shallot and herbs and season to taste.

Preheat an oven-top griddle pan over a medium-high heat. Rub the pigeon breasts with the olive oil and lightly season. Cook on the griddle pan for 3 minutes on each side until seared but still pink inside. Remove and marinate thoroughly in the honey dressing. Once cool, cover and chill in the dressing for a minimum of 12 hours.

When ready to serve, drop the beans into boiling water and cook for 8 minutes or until very tender. Drain and leave to drip dry in a colander.

In a large bowl, whisk together 2 tablespoons white wine vinegar with the garlic, 6 tablespoons walnut oil, salt and freshly ground black pepper. Add to the cooked green beans with the walnuts and salad leaves and toss. Finely slice each pigeon breast (discard the marinade) and gently mix into the salad. Divide between four plates and serve immediately.

## CRISPY FRIED SQUID WITH LEMON VERBENA DIP

One of the most direct methods of imbuing a dish with a herbal flavour is to accompany it with a herbal sauce. Pesto is a classic and somewhat overused example, but there are many other types of sauces that can be used. Raw herbs release the most flavour. The key is to add an element of surprise by selecting an unexpected herb. Naturally, it has to taste good. Here, I've infused a Thai-style sweet and sour sauce with some lemon verbena to add subtle fresh herbal notes to the squid. If you can't get hold of lemon verbena, use the same quantity of lemon balm or 2 teaspoons of finely chopped lemon thyme. Ask the fishmonger to clean the squid for you.

---

**SERVES 4**

2 tablespoons granulated sugar

½ teaspoon dried chilli flakes

2½ tablespoons white wine vinegar

4 tablespoons finely chopped lemon verbena leaves

800 g uncleaned weight, or 500 g cleaned weight, fresh squid

corn oil for deep frying

50 g plain flour

salt and freshly ground black pepper

To make the dip, mix together the sugar, dried chilli flakes and 5 tablespoons boiling water. Stir until the sugar has melted. Add the vinegar, followed by the lemon verbena. Set aside.

Rinse the cleaned squid bodies inside and out under the cold tap, making sure that any sand or gloopy bits are washed away. Slice into thick rounds.

Trim the tentacles so that they are just held together by a ring of flesh. Rinse and if you don't like the suckers, scrape them off with the blunt side of a knife. Dry both the squid rings and tentacles on kitchen paper. If they're not dry, too much flour will adhere to them and they're liable to spit in the hot oil. Cover and chill until needed.

Half fill a deep-fat fryer or one third fill a deep pan with oil. For the latter, clip a thermometer on to the side of the pan. Heat the oil to 180°C. Put the flour in a large mixing bowl and season with salt and freshly ground black pepper. Mix in one-third to a quarter of the squid, then shake off the excess flour before adding to the hot oil. Fry for about 3 minutes or until golden, remove and drain thoroughly on kitchen paper. Place in a bowl. Repeat the process with the remaining squid. Season to taste with salt and serve a pile of golden squid on each plate with a little bowl of dip.

## NASTURTIUM AND CHIVE BUTTER TAGLIATELLE

Smell, like all our senses, is subjective. Consequently, categories are bound to vary from one person to another. For me, the dominant aroma of a nasturtium is not 'floral' but 'herbal', hence its place in this chapter. Herbs combined with dairy products or oils will instantly create an emotional impact when eaten with a subtle-tasting food such as pasta or bread.

**SERVES 2**

**185 g tagliatelle**

**salt**

**1 small organic lemon**

**55 g unsalted butter, softened**

**1 small bunch chives, finely sliced**

**3 handfuls nasturtium flowers, finely sliced**

**½ red Thai chilli (or to taste), finely sliced**

**freshly ground black pepper**

**2 tablespoons finely grated Parmesan**

Cook the tagliatelle in plenty of boiling salted water according to the instructions on the packet. Meanwhile, finely grate the lemon and place the zest in a bowl with the butter, chives, nasturtium flowers and chilli. Beat vigorously until amalgamated and set aside.

Roughly drain the pasta in a colander and return to the pan. Add the nasturtium butter, a twist of freshly ground black pepper and about a tablespoon of lemon juice. Mix thoroughly until the butter has melted and the tagliatelle is well coated. Season to taste, adjusting the lemon juice if necessary. Serve immediately with some freshly grated Parmesan.

# WILD MUSHROOM HERB TART

Any summer mushrooms, such as chanterelles *Cantharellus cibarius*, saffron milk caps *Lactarius deliciosus*, ceps *Boletus edulis* or field mushrooms *Agaricus campestris* are delicious in this recipe. The herbal notes of tarragon and parsley add a light summery green note that negates the potentially musty flavour of the mushrooms. Remove the herbs and add some smoked ham and your tart takes on autumnal flavours.

**SERVES 6**

**225 g shortcrust pastry (see page 169)**

**3 tablespoons olive oil**

**1 onion, finely diced**

**250 g wild mushrooms, trimmed and wiped**

**2 large handfuls flat leaf parsley, finely chopped**

**1 teaspoon finely chopped tarragon**

**salt and freshly ground black pepper**

**1 medium egg**

**1 medium egg yolk**

**200 ml double cream**

**20 g finely grated Gruyère**

Roll the pastry out on a lightly floured surface and use to line a 23 cm diameter tart case. Prick the base, line with greaseproof paper and fill with baking beans. Chill for 30 minutes.

Preheat the oven to Gas Mark 4/180°C and bake the pastry case for 15 minutes. Once cool enough to handle, remove the beans and paper.

Set a frying pan over a medium-low heat. Add the oil and, once hot, sauté the onion for 10 minutes or until soft. Roughly slice or rip the mushrooms and stir into the onion. Increase the heat slightly and cook briskly for 5 minutes or until the mushrooms are lightly cooked and any excess liquid has evaporated. Remove from the heat, mix in the herbs and season to taste.

Beat together the eggs and cream. Mix in the sautéed mushrooms and adjust the seasoning to taste. Tip into the pastry case, sprinkle with the cheese and immediately return to the oven. Bake for 30 minutes or until golden and slightly risen. Serve hot, warm or cold.

## LAMB KOFTA, PITTA AND HERB SALAD

For most cooks, it is second nature to add herbs to fish and meat, either in the form of a marinade or as a seasoning. However, subjecting a herb to heat will reduce its potency. One way of re-establishing its fresh flavour is to serve the same herb raw with the cooked dish. It might be in the form of a garnish, vegetable or salad. Here, for example, a few leaves of coriander are slipped into the salad that accompanies the coriander-flavoured lamb koftas. This technique can be applied to other salads or accompanying vegetables.

Amchoor powder is the dried and ground pulp of sour mangos. It can be found in Asian shops. Gram flour is made from chickpeas and is sold in some supermarkets, as well as Asian shops.

---

**SERVES 4**

1 large bunch coriander

2 medium onions, roughly diced

1 tablespoon finely chopped fresh ginger

200 g natural Greek yoghurt

1½ tablespoons amchoor powder or lemon juice

1 teaspoon garam masala

½ teaspoon chilli powder

1 tablespoon gram flour (optional)

salt

500 g lean minced lamb

1 teaspoon sunflower oil

½ teaspoon cumin seeds

1 cucumber, peeled

130 g mixed baby salad leaves

2 red onions, finely sliced

8 pitta breads

1½ tablespoons lemon juice

2 tablespoons extra virgin olive oil

To make the kebabs, strip the leaves from the coriander. Place all but a handful in a food processor. Add the diced onions, ginger, 3 tablespoons yoghurt, the amchoor powder or lemon juice, garam masala, chilli powder, gram flour and 2 teaspoons of salt. Process in short bursts until the mixture forms a paste, then add the minced lamb. Whiz briefly to give the meat a smoother texture, then tip into a bowl. Mix thoroughly and divide into 12 equal portions.

Line a tray with foil and lightly grease with sunflower oil. Roll the portions into smooth, even-sized sausages and place on the tray. Cover and chill until needed.

Whisk the remaining yoghurt with 100 ml water and season to taste with salt. Lightly toast the cumin seeds in a dry frying pan over a medium heat for 2 minutes or until they begin to colour, then remove and grind to a powder using a pestle and mortar or rolling pin. Sprinkle over the yoghurt sauce.

Halve the cucumber lengthwise and finely slice. Place in a large bowl with the salad leaves, remaining coriander leaves and sliced red onions. Cover and chill until needed.

Preheat the grill to high. Cook the kebabs under the grill for 10 minutes, turning once, until they are cooked through. Toast the pitta breads for about a minute on each side or until hot but not crispy. Split each bread open along one side. Add the lemon juice and olive oil to the salad mixture and season to taste. Stuff the salad into the pitta breads before topping each with one and a half kebabs and drizzling with yoghurt. Serve immediately with plenty of napkins to hand.

# BASIL FRUIT SALAD

Herbs infused into sugar syrups add a complex, scented note to sorbets, salads, poached fruit and cakes that takes the eater unawares. A sudden taste of crushed basil, for example, might evoke sea breezes and lazy lunches on the Ligurian coast. Experiment with other herbs such as tarragon, thyme, fennel, lemon verbena, bay and scented pelargoniums.

**SERVES 4**

**zest and juice from 1 organic lemon**

**3 sprigs basil, plus a few extra leaves**

**115 g granulated sugar**

**2 ripe peaches, peeled, stoned and quartered**

**300 g strawberries, hulled and halved**

**250 g cherries, halved and stoned**

**250 g raspberries**

Finely pare the zest from the lemon and place in a small non-corrosive saucepan with the basil, 285 ml water and the sugar. Dissolve the sugar over a low heat, then simmer for 10 minutes.

Remove the basil syrup from the heat and add the lemon juice. Set aside to cool slightly – about 20 minutes.

Halve each peach quarter and place in a pretty bowl. Mix the strawberries into the peaches with the cherries and raspberries. Remove the basil from the warm syrup and pour the syrup over the fruit. Mix thoroughly and serve scattered with a few basil leaves. Don't chill as this reduces the fragrance of the basil.

## ROSEMARY MERINGUES WITH CRUSHED RASPBERRY CREAM

Old fashioned 'sweet' herbs such as rosemary, thyme, marjoram, basil and tarragon are enjoying a renaissance in Britain as a flavouring for sweet dishes such as meringues, syllabubs and custards.

**SERVES 8**

**3 medium egg whites**

**170 g caster sugar**

**½ tablespoon cornflour**

**1 tablespoon finely chopped fresh rosemary**

**1 teaspoon white wine vinegar**

**285 ml double cream, whipped**

**1 tablespoon icing sugar (or to taste)**

**5 tablespoons apple juice**

**2 tablespoons Calvados**

**400 g raspberries**

Preheat the oven to Gas Mark 1/140°C. Line two baking trays with baking paper.

Put the egg whites in a large, clean, dry bowl and whisk until they form stiff peaks. Add a quarter of the caster sugar and whisk until the mixture is stiff and glossy, then gradually whisk in the remaining sugar until the mixture is very glossy. Finally, fold in the cornflour, rosemary and vinegar.

Spoon eight evenly spaced blobs of meringue on to each paper-covered tray so that you have 16 meringues. Place in the oven and bake for 15 minutes. Reduce the heat to Gas Mark ½/130°C and cook for a further 30 minutes or until the meringues are crisp outside and gooey inside. Remove from the oven, peel the meringues off the paper and leave until cold on a cake rack.

Whip the cream with the icing sugar, apple juice and Calvados until it forms soft peaks. Mix in the raspberries so that they are slightly crushed and colour the cream in pink streaks. Serve two meringues with every helping of raspberry cream.

# LEMON THYME DRIZZLE CAKE

Herbs can be used like spices to flavour cake and pudding batters. In this recipe, the cake is drenched in lemon juice mixed with fresh lemon thyme and sugar to reinforce the fragile scent of lemon thyme in the cake batter.

This method can be adapted to floral flavourings such as lavender, rose and jasmine. You could also replace the crunchy topping with a normal lemon icing flavoured with finely chopped herbs. This cake keeps well if wrapped in foil.

**SERVES 8**

**115 g unsalted butter, softened, plus extra for greasing**

**2 bunches lemon thyme**

**140 g granulated sugar**

**175 g caster sugar**

**finely grated zest and juice of 2 lemons**

**3 medium eggs, beaten**

**175 g self-raising flour, sifted**

Preheat the oven to Gas Mark 4/180°C. Cut out a circle of baking paper to fit the base of a 20-cm cake tin with a removable base. Lightly butter the tin, line the base with the paper and lightly grease the paper.

Wash and dry the lemon thyme thoroughly. Strip the leaves from their stems and finely chop. Mix half the chopped thyme into the granulated sugar and set aside. Beat the remaining thyme with the butter, caster sugar and lemon zest until the mixture is pale and fluffy.

Using a wooden spoon, beat in one third of the eggs, followed by one third of the flour. Repeat until all the eggs and flour are incorporated, then beat in 4 tablespoons of lemon juice. Spoon the mixture into the cake tin. Level the surface and bake in the oven for 35 minutes or until a knife comes out clean when inserted into the cake. The cake is cooked when the surface springs back when lightly pressed and the sides have shrunk slightly from the tin.

Remove the cake from the oven. Quickly mix the remaining lemon juice into the granulated sugar mixture and pour over the piping hot surface of the cake. Once the cake is cool enough to handle, remove from its tin and peel away the paper from its base. Leave to cool crunchy side up on a cake rack.

# AUGUST FRUIT

# SUGARY PLUMS BUBBLING IN A JAM PAN

Fruit, perhaps more than any other food, still resonates with our primitive past. Consider the intense pleasure experienced when eating sweet juicy cherries or biting into a fragrant peach. The hum of industrial life momentarily fades as a wave of pure enjoyment sweeps through the eater, encouraging us to take another bite of fruit. Some scientists suggest that the musky sweet notes of many fruit flavours, such as blackberries, are akin to the pheromones that we detect suckling at our mother's breast; others believe that the smell of warm sugary fruit (like hot strawberry jam) rekindles childhood memories of boiled sweets and childish puddings. Whatever the truth, it would seem that fruit flavours usually provoke a favourable, warm feeling in the eater.

Within each fruit lie many different aromas depending on how you prepare it. A freshly picked fig is redolent of honey and sap, but bake it for a few minutes and its flavour turns to musk and wine, while poaching seems to bring out more floral notes.

The sublest aromas are experienced when eating fruit raw. These fade gradually after the fruit is picked. Hence, the exquisite flavour of blackberries gathered from a sunny hedgerow. The best cooks serve such food simply; either at room temperature or with the slight chill of an old-fashioned, stone-shelved pantry, so that the eater can appreciate the fine flavour unadulterated. Wild blackberries with sugar and cream, for example, or, as Edward Bunyard suggests in his enjoyably opinionated *The Anatomy of Dessert* (1933), ripe greengages with nothing other than a glass of chilled Hock.

However, the delicate floral and citrus aromas in fresh fruit can also add an appealing depth of flavour to savoury salads and salsas, especially when combined with lime juice and fresh chilli. A lime, olive oil and chilli-dressed romaine leaf salad, for instance, tastes sublime when you add sliced peaches with a few slices of red onion and some crumbled Feta.

Cooking or drying fruit creates richer, deeper aromas. These can be exploited in the most delicious ways by layering with other flavours. Thus, the intense taste of cooked blackcurrants can be played with by combining them with the herbal creamy flavours of a rosemary-infused custard to create a magical summer Blackcurrant rosemary fool (see page 109). Or you might layer different fruit flavours together, such as with a buttery baked peach and raspberry sponge pudding, perhaps spiked with a vanilla pod as in Eve's summer pudding (see page 110). The complex fruity notes of a richly spiced fruit chutney takes this concept to its furthest point.

Your personality and memories will dictate how you utilise such flavours. For me, August is the month in which fruit adds a pensive note to my food. Luscious colours and rich fragrances hint at autumn, despite the deserted hot pavements of London streets.

# CHILLED ROASTED TOMATO SOUP

The simplest way to deepen the flavour of fruit such as tomatoes is to roast them, as this intensifies the sugars and adds subtle caramel notes. This soup freezes well and is also good served hot.

**SERVES 6**

4 tablespoons extra virgin olive oil

2 onions, very thickly sliced

4 carrots, peeled and thickly sliced

2 sticks celery, thickly sliced

4 cloves garlic, peeled

1.5 kg ripe tomatoes

6 sprigs lemon thyme

3 stems parsley

450 ml good chicken stock (see page 168)

salt and freshly ground black pepper

150 ml double cream

½ small bunch chives, snipped

Preheat the oven to Gas Mark 4/180°C. Pour the oil into a large non-stick roasting tray and toss in the onions, carrots, celery, garlic and whole tomatoes. Slip the thyme and parsley under the tomatoes so that they don't burn as the vegetables cook. Roast in the centre of the oven for 1½ hours or until the vegetables are soft and golden.

Discard the thyme sprigs, add the chicken stock to the vegetables and deglaze the roasting tray. Scrape everything into a large saucepan, add 400 ml water and gently boil for 15 minutes. Purée in a blender and strain into a clean container. Adjust the seasoning to taste, cover and chill until cold.

To serve, divide between six bowls. Pour a pretty swirl of double cream on top of each serving, sprinkle with chives and serve.

## SPICED SWORDFISH SALAD

Raw fruit notes can introduce an intriguing note to recipes. Here, the complex sweet flavour of fresh peaches offsets the smokiness of the fish to create a fascinating dish that compels the eater into taking another bite. You can substitute the peaches with nectarines, mango or even pineapple.

**SERVES 4**

4 x 200 g swordfish steaks

2 tablespoons sweet smoked paprika

2 teaspoons dried garlic granules

salt and freshly ground black pepper

5 tablespoons extra virgin olive oil

2 romaine lettuce hearts

100 g mixed wild rocket and red chard

generous handful coriander leaves

1 small Thai chilli, finely sliced

1 cucumber, peeled, halved and sliced

1 small red onion, finely sliced

3 ripe yellow peaches or nectarines

juice of 2 limes

Preheat an oven-top griddle pan over a medium heat. Trim the swordfish steaks of any skin and dark reddish flesh. Mix together the paprika, garlic granules, salt and pepper. Lightly coat the swordfish in 3 tablespoons oil, then rub in the spice mixture.

Tear the lettuce hearts into pieces and place in a large salad bowl with the rocket, chard and coriander leaves. Add the sliced chilli, cucumber and red onion. Quarter and stone the peaches or nectarines. (There is no need to peel them.) Slice each quarter and add to the salad leaves.

Place the spiced swordfish on the hot griddle pan. Cook for 4–5 minutes on each side or until cooked through and juicy – but not pink – in the middle. The cooking time will vary according to the thickness of your fish. Remove to a plate and season with 3 tablespoons of lime juice.

Season the salad with salt and pepper, add 3 tablespoons of lime juice and 2 tablespoons olive oil and mix thoroughly. Divide between four plates. Roughly break up the warm swordfish steaks and tuck the chunks into the salad. Serve immediately.

## ROAST FIGS WITH FETA, FENNEL AND ROCKET SALAD

Fresh figs have a complex fruity, floral aroma that is enriched and deepened by cooking. Their luscious summery scent is further enhanced here by combining them with the floral notes of fennel and creamy tones of a barrel-cured Feta cheese to create a heavenly light lunch.

**SERVES 4**

**1 teaspoon walnut oil, plus a further 3 tablespoons**

**8 ripe figs**

**2 tablespoons lemon juice**

**2 plump heads Florence fennel**

**50 g wild rocket**

**salt and freshly ground black pepper**

**225 g barrel-cured Feta cheese**

Preheat the oven to Gas Mark 6/200°C. Lightly oil a small baking dish with 1 teaspoon walnut oil. Trim the stalk of each fig and arrange snugly in the baking dish. Drizzle with 1 tablespoon lemon juice and bake in the preheated oven for 20 minutes or until soft and oozing with juice.

Meanwhile, trim and halve the fennel, discarding the tough outer layers. Finely slice the inner layers into almost transparent fans and place in a large mixing bowl. Add the rocket leaves.

Once the figs are cooked, remove from the oven and allow to cool for about 10 minutes. When you are ready to serve, dress the salad with 1 tablespoon lemon juice and 3 tablespoons of walnut oil. Season to taste and arrange in airy piles on four plates. Tuck two figs into each salad, gently splitting them open as you do so. Crumble the Feta into chunks and scatter around the salad. Spoon any fig juices over the cheese and figs. Serve with walnut bread if wished.

## SPICED RED CABBAGE COLESLAW

The first apples of the season have what Edward Bunyard categorised as 'the Strawberry or Raspberry flavour', Worcester Pearmain being the most obvious example of the latter. Their scented aroma and fresh sweet-sour taste is exquisite when combined with lime, mint and chilli in this simple salad.

**SERVES 4**

¼ red cabbage (about 450 g)

2 carrots, peeled

1 bunch chives, finely snipped

a large handful mint leaves, roughly sliced

½ Thai chilli (or to taste), finely sliced

1 tablespoon lime juice

3 tablespoons extra virgin olive oil

2 early dessert apples, such as Worcester Pearmain or Discovery

salt and freshly ground black pepper

Trim the cabbage and remove the tough outer leaves. Wash and halve, removing the tough white core. Finely slice the remainder and place in a large mixing bowl.

Cut the carrots into fine matchsticks about 5 cm in length. Add to the cabbage with the chives, mint, chilli, lime juice and olive oil.

Quarter, core and finely slice the apples. Mix into the salad and season to taste. Serve when ready.

## BARBECUED PORK WITH CHINESE SPICED PLUM SAUCE

Cooked fruit sauces are used as an accompaniment to savoury dishes around the world. Each country devises flavours that enhance their ingredients and reflect their environment. Thus the Chinese grow a different variety of plum, *Prunus mume*, to the British and pickle them half ripe in salt and sugar before drying them and turning them into sauce. In Xinjiang Province in northern China these trees grow as tall as sycamores, their rustling leaves offering welcome shade in the dusty summer heat. The piquant flavour of their fruit mirrors the intense earthy spicy aromas that pervade China's towns. British food requires softer flavours to echo the smells of our natural environment – be it sun-baked London pavements or freshly harvested cornfields. Hence this very British recipe for home-grown plum sauce.

I use Mizkan, a brand of Japanese rice vinegar, in much of my cooking. It has a delicate taste and is available from Japanese shops. This recipe is particularly good served with a pilaff and blanched spinach warmed with sautéed garlic.

**SERVES 4**

**700 g trimmed organic pork loin fillet**

**For the marinade:**

**1 red chilli, finely chopped**

**1 clove garlic, finely chopped**

**1 teaspoon finely chopped ginger**

**1½ tablespoons Kikkoman soy sauce**

**1 tablespoon rice (or white wine) vinegar**

**2 tablespoons toasted sesame oil**

**For the sauce:**

**300 g plums, such as Reeves or Victoria, quartered and stoned**

**½ red Thai chilli (or to taste), roughly sliced**

**1 teaspoon finely diced ginger**

**1 star anise**

**55 g granulated sugar**

**3 tablespoons rice (or white wine) vinegar**

Begin with the marinade. Mix together the chilli, garlic, ginger, soy sauce, vinegar and sesame oil in a large bowl. Trim the pork fillet of any fat, cut into four evenly sized pieces and coat in the marinade. Cover and chill for 3 hours.

To make the sauce, place the plums in a non-corrosive saucepan with the chilli, ginger, star anise, granulated sugar, vinegar and 3 tablespoons of water. Set over a medium heat and stir occasionally until the sugar has dissolved, then simmer gently for 30 minutes. Remove the star anise and purée the sauce. Set aside until needed.

Further cut the pork into 2 cm-thick rounds and re-coat in the marinade. Light a barbecue and, once the coals are grey and glowing red, grill for 3–4 minutes on each side, or until cooked through. If you don't have a barbecue or it's a rainy day, use an oven-top griddle pan. When cut open, the meat should be juicy but no longer be pink. Heat the plum sauce until warm rather than hot and serve with the pork.

## DUCK BREASTS WITH CHERRY SAUCE

Textured fruit sauces, such as the cherry sauce here, will immediately give the eater a more intense experience since the fruit releases its rich 'cooked' flavour as it is chewed. English dessert cherries are available in July and August, and morello cherries appear in August. As they are hard to find, I have used dessert cherries in this recipe. It relies on the reduction of a flavoursome stock to give it a rich umami taste that then adds depth to the lighter fruity notes of the cherries, redcurrant jelly and orange zest.

**SERVES 6**

**1.2 litres homemade duck or chicken stock (see page 168)**

**300 ml fruity red wine, such as Pinot Noir**

**3 strips finely pared orange zest**

**3 tablespoons redcurrant jelly**

**3 tablespoons port**

**340 g fresh red cherries, halved and stoned**

**6 x 225 g duck breasts with skin on**

**salt and freshly ground black pepper**

The base of the sauce can be made the day before if wished. Pour the stock into a non-corrosive saucepan. Boil vigorously until it has reduced down to about 150 ml. It should have a lovely meaty flavour. Add the red wine and orange zest and boil until it has again reduced down to 150 ml. Stir in the redcurrant jelly and port and simmer until the jelly has dissolved. Chill now, or continue by transferring to a smaller non-corrosive saucepan. Bring up to the boil and add the cherries. Simmer for 3 minutes then remove from the heat.

Preheat the oven to Gas Mark 6/200°C. Trim the duck breasts of any sinews or bloody areas and score the skin in a diamond pattern. Liberally salt the breasts on both sides before lightly peppering.

Heat a dry, non-stick frying pan over a medium heat. Once hot, place three of the duck breasts skin-side down in the hot pan. As soon as the fat turns golden brown, after about 2 minutes, turn the pieces over to sear the flesh. Transfer flesh-side down to a non-stick roasting tray. Pour the duck fat into a small bowl; it's perfect for roasting potatoes. Repeat the process with the remaining duck breasts.

Roast the duck breasts in the preheated oven for 10 minutes. Remove and allow to rest in a warm place for a further 5 minutes. Reheat the sauce over a low heat and season to taste. Carve the duck into thick slices and serve with the hot cherry sauce.

# BLACKCURRANT ROSEMARY FOOL

On a hot August day there are few things as wonderful as allowing the flavour of blackcurrants and custard to melt in your mouth. The rosemary adds an unexpected summery fragrance. This recipe can be turned into ice cream by freezing and churning the mixture.

**SERVES 4**

**250 g blackcurrants**

**285 ml double cream**

**3 large sprigs rosemary**

**225 g caster sugar**

**4 medium egg yolks**

Strip the blackcurrants from their stems and place them in a small non-corrosive saucepan. Set over a low heat until they start to release their juice, stirring occasionally, then simmer until they are swimming in juice. This will take about 15 minutes in all.

Meanwhile, put the cream and rosemary sprigs into a saucepan. Set over a low heat and slowly bring up to the boil. Set aside to infuse for 20 minutes.

Mix half the sugar into the hot blackcurrants, stir until dissolved, then remove the pan from the heat and push the juicy currants through a sieve into a bowl. Discard the pips.

Whisk the egg yolks and remaining sugar together in a mixing bowl until thick and pale. Gradually beat the infused rosemary cream, sprigs and all, into the egg yolks. Return the mixture to the saucepan. Set over a low heat, stirring continuously with a wooden spoon until it forms a thick custard. This will take about 20 minutes. Do not let it boil. If you think the custard is becoming too hot, remove the pan from the heat and keep stirring briskly. Once it has cooled slightly, return it to the heat. You must not stop stirring or leave the custard unattended during this stage as it can easily split. The custard should be thick enough to liberally coat the back of the spoon.

Remove the custard from the heat and strain into the blackcurrant purée. Discard the rosemary. Mix thoroughly and lightly cover until cool. When cooled, chill until the custard thickens into a luscious fool. Remove from the fridge about 30 minutes before serving. Spoon into individual glasses or bowls and serve cool but not icy cold to maximise its herbal flavour.

## EVE'S SUMMER PUDDING

Combining different fruit flavours can create evocative puddings. The classic combination of raspberries and nectarines or peaches are mixed here in a sponge-topped pudding with strawberries and vanilla. Freshly baked, its smell conjures up hot raspberry jam and school holidays.

**SERVES 6**

650 g ripe nectarines or peaches

115 g granulated sugar (or to taste)

250 g strawberries

400 g raspberries

1 vanilla pod, split open

115 g unsalted butter, softened

115 g caster sugar, plus extra for sprinkling

2 medium eggs

115 g self-raising flour

Preheat the oven to Gas Mark 4/180°C. Peel the nectarines or peaches. If they are slightly unripe, cut a small cross on the base and cover with boiling water before slipping off the skins. Quarter, stone and cut into medium-sized chunks. Mix with the granulated sugar in a large bowl.

Wash, hull and halve the strawberries. Mix into the nectarines or peaches with the raspberries. Tip into a deep pie dish and tuck the vanilla pod into the middle of the fruit.

Beat the butter and caster sugar together until fluffy. Beat in the eggs, one at a time, followed by the flour. Spoon blobs of the mixture on to the peaches and roughly spread over the fruit. Place the pie dish in the centre of the oven immediately. Bake for 50 minutes or until golden and risen into a layer of springy sponge. The underside will be soft because of the fruit juices.

Remove from the oven and sprinkle with extra caster sugar. Serve warm or at room temperature with lots of cream.

# SEPTEMBER FUNGI

## DAMP LEAVES UNDERFOOT

There are certain flavours that act as powerful undertones in cooking, and fungic aromas belong to this category. They have a dusky, feral scent that can add a subtle, wild edge to a dish if used in moderation, be it a mushroom pizza flecked with goat's cheese or pears baked with blue cheese and served with peppery watercress leaves. This sense of wildness can be further enhanced by careful design in a recipe. The autumnal feel of sautéed chanterelles in a creamy tart, for example, can be echoed with a salad of wild leaves and herbs. Subconsciously, such ideas capture the eater's psyche, so that they too feel at one with the natural world. However, take care not to over-do fungic flavours and slimy mushroom textures, as they can also create unpleasant associations such

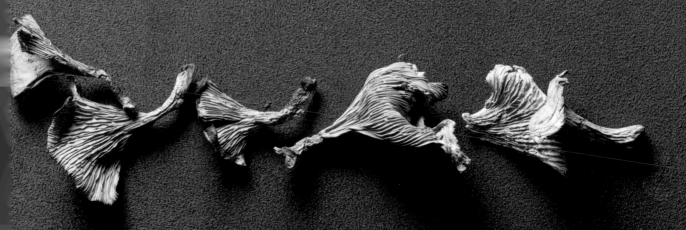

as the whiff of the wine cellar with its damp mould, dusty cobwebs and spiders lurking in the darkness.

There is an odd pleasure in sniffing things. It becomes irresistible to unwrap the wax paper around a wedge of mature cheddar just so you can snuffle the cheese before rewrapping and storing it. As your senses become more refined, you will pick up the musty scent of air-dried ham when you walk into an Italian delicatessen, or the exquisite aroma of white truffle being freshly shaved on to warm pasta at a neighbouring restaurant table.

Early autumn is perhaps the best time to cultivate your sensitivity to fungic flavours. Cool damp nights and early morning mists smell of water-soaked fallen vegetation, rotting wood, moss and wild mushrooms that gradually fades with the warmth of the day. It is the smell of dough rising in a bowl in a warm kitchen, and the aromatic scent of beer frothing over the top of a pint glass in a fuggy pub. The more you sniff, the more you will become aware of yeasty, fungic smells, some pleasant, others less so.

Curiously, many chefs have a peculiar partiality to fungic flavours. Perhaps this is because they love cooking with umami-rich ingredients. These foods have a strong savoury, moreish taste, such as you find in Parmesan, peas and seared scallops. Many umami-tasting foods also have a fungic aroma, for example, ripe cheese, cured meats and dried shitake mushrooms. Since umami naturally enhances the sweetness and the saltiness in a dish, it is important to use such ingredients lightly, or at least to counterbalance them with a little acidity, otherwise they can taste cloying. Add a few citrus, herbal or buttery notes and you will create a divine dish.

## MADEIRA MUSHROOM BROTH WITH CHIVES

Open a packet of dried ceps and inhale deeply. An intense velvety mushroom aroma will temporarily flood your senses, hence the need for so few ingredients in this simple soup. Since the mushroom aroma is so strong here, I've kept the texture of the soup very light, adding chives for a splash of herbal freshness.

**SERVES 6**

**75 g dried ceps**

**1.5 litres good chicken stock (see page 168)**

**600 g button mushrooms, trimmed**

**3 tablespoons olive oil**

**6 tablespoons Madeira**

**3 small bunches chives, finely sliced**

**sea salt**

Rinse the ceps under the tap then place them in a large bowl. Heat the stock and pour half of it over the dried ceps. Leave them to soak for 20 minutes.

Slice the button mushrooms. Heat the oil in a non-corrosive saucepan over a high heat. Add the button mushrooms and stir fry briskly for 2–3 minutes. Once they begin to release their liquid, add the ceps and all the chicken stock. Bring up to the boil and simmer gently for about 7 minutes. Add the Madeira and chives, season to taste and serve.

## HOMEMADE PIZZA DOUGH

Uncooked pizza dough freezes very well, so I usually triple the amount and freeze two thirds so that I can throw together a pizza at a moment's notice.

**MAKES 3 PIZZAS, EACH OF WHICH SERVES 2**
**3 teaspoons dried yeast**
**675 g plain flour**
**1½ teaspoons salt**
**170 ml full fat milk**
**2½ tablespoons extra virgin olive oil**

Measure 300 ml tepid water into a small bowl and sprinkle the yeast over the top. Leave for 10 minutes or until it has dissolved and the water smells of fresh yeast and looks active.

Place the flour and salt in a mixing bowl. Stir in the yeast water. Rinse the yeast bowl with the milk and tip into the flour. Using your hands, mix together until it all forms a soft, pliant dough. Turn out on to a clean surface and knead thoroughly for 5–10 minutes or until it feels silky smooth. Roughly flatten it and make a few indentations with your fingertips. Pour over 2 tablespoons olive oil and fold the dough over, kneading carefully until the oil is absorbed. Initially, it will be very squelchy.

Pour ½ tablespoon olive oil into a large clean bowl. Shape the dough into a ball, place in the bowl, roll in the oil and cover with cling film. Leave in a warm place for 2 hours or until the dough has doubled in size.

Divide the dough into three even-sized portions. If using straight away, lightly cover each portion with cling film until you are ready to roll it out. If keeping for another time, slip each one into a small polythene bag and freeze until needed.

## ARTICHOKE AND PROSCIUTTO PIZZA

I would categorise the smell of yeast as fungic. It changes according to the ingredients in your dough and becomes most subtle once cooked. Add buckwheat flour to your dough and it will smell more yeasty, while dough made with plain white flour has the faintest of fungic scents. This aroma can be enhanced or lessened in a pizza, depending on your choice of topping. Blue cheese or sautéed wild mushrooms would emphasise such flavours, whereas tomatoes would negate it. Here, I've chosen the earthy flavour of artichoke hearts mixed with creamy notes of mozzarella. The prosciutto and Parmesan cheese adds an extra umami kick.

**SERVES 2 AS A MAIN COURSE**

**1 onion, sliced into thick rings**

**1 tablespoon extra virgin olive oil**

**salt and freshly ground black pepper**

**3 preserved artichoke hearts**

**⅓ quantity pizza dough (see opposite)**

**80 g finely sliced Prosciutto di Parma**

**1 buffalo mozzarella, sliced**

**30 g Parmesan cheese, finely grated**

Preheat the oven to Gas Mark 7/220°C. Place a heavy baking sheet on both the bottom and middle shelf. You will also need the bases of two 20-cm diameter non-stick cake tins.

Preheat an oven-top griddle pan. Coat the onion rings in the olive oil, then season with salt and pepper. Arrange in a single layer on the griddle pan and cook for 3 minutes on each side or until softened and caramelised. Tip into a bowl and set aside. Halve the artichoke hearts, rinse under a warm tap and pat dry on kitchen paper. Mix into the onions.

Divide the dough into two even-sized balls. Roll the first ball into a rough disc shape and place on one of the cake tin bases before rolling it into the same sized circle as the tin base. Repeat the process with the second ball. Cover each pizza with half the onion and artichoke mixture. Top each with ripped slices of Parma ham, followed by the sliced mozzarella. Sprinkle with the Parmesan and place each pizza on its own baking sheet in the oven. Bake for about 15 minutes or until the cheese is melted and flecked gold and the crust is crisp and golden. Remove and slip on to plates.

## LAMB BURGER WITH BLUE CHEESE BUTTER

Blue cheese butter adds an interesting slightly 'wild' fungic note to grilled meats such as steak or lamb. Since it also has a strong umami taste, it will automatically make the meat taste sweeter. To play with the concept of wild food, serve with a salad that contains bitter salad leaves, such as rocket and watercress. Hungry guests might appreciate it squashed between two slices of grilled bread with a hint of lettuce, but if you want to be utterly adored by those you are feeding, add a portion of home-made salted Chips (see page 133).

**SERVES 4**

2 tablespoons extra virgin olive oil

2 shallots, finely diced

1 clove garlic, finely diced

1 small bunch parsley

a handful lemon thyme

finely grated zest from 1 lemon

500 g lean minced lamb

salt and freshly ground black pepper

30 g unsalted butter, softened

30 g Roquefort or Stilton

2 tablespoons finely sliced chives

To make the burgers, heat 1 tablespoon oil in a small frying pan and fry the shallots and garlic for 8 minutes or until soft. Finely chop the leaves from the parsley and lemon thyme. Tip into a bowl and mix in the lemon zest, minced lamb, softened shallots, salt and pepper. Fry a nugget of the mix and taste to test the seasoning. When you are happy, shape and mix into four burgers. Cover and chill until needed.

Make the blue cheese butter by beating together the softened butter and blue cheese. Once well mixed, beat in the chives and season to taste with black pepper. If wished, form into a sausage on some greaseproof paper. Roll up the paper and gently roll under your fingertips until the butter forms a smooth cylinder. Chill until needed.

Preheat an oven-top griddle pan over a medium-high heat. When ready to eat, brush the burgers with 1 tablespoon olive oil and grill for 6 or 7 minutes on each side for medium-well cooked burgers. Slice the butter into rounds, place on the hot burgers and serve immediately.

# CHANTERELLE AND CHILLI TAGLIATELLE

The scent of chanterelles sizzling with garlic, shallots and chilli immediately conjures up early autumn evenings for me. Steam billows from the strained pasta, butter melts and the aromas blend to create the perfect TV supper that hints at falling autumn leaves. Winter is coming.

**SERVES 2**

**200 g chanterelle mushrooms**

**5 slices smoked back bacon (optional)**

**175 g dried tagliatelle**

**salt**

**3 tablespoons extra virgin olive oil**

**1 small clove garlic, finely diced**

**½ teaspoon dried chilli flakes**

**1 tablespoon lemon juice**

**a handful flat leaf parsley leaves, roughly chopped**

**30 g unsalted butter**

**freshly ground black pepper**

**freshly grated Parmesan to serve**

Wash and trim the chanterelles. Pat dry on kitchen paper, halve or quarter any large ones and set them all aside. Trim the bacon (if using) of fat and cut into small strips.

Drop the pasta into a saucepan of boiling salted water. Cook until it is al dente – the time will vary according to the brand of the pasta but it is usually around 10 minutes.

Set a frying pan over a medium-high heat. Add the oil and, once hot, add the bacon. Stir fry briskly for 3 minutes or until lightly coloured, then reduce the heat to low and stir in the garlic and chilli flakes. Fry gently for 1–2 minutes, then mix in the mushrooms and increase the heat.

Fry briskly, stirring regularly for 3 minutes or until the mushrooms are tender. Don't worry if they release a lot of juice, just continue to cook until the liquid has evaporated. Add the lemon juice and parsley, quickly swirl in half the butter and season to taste.

Meanwhile, drain the pasta, shake briefly and return to the saucepan. Add the remaining butter, season with black pepper and stir until the butter has melted. Immediately mix in the mushrooms. Divide between two plates and serve with freshly grated Parmesan cheese.

# BEEF WITH BEER

Beer adds a subtle yeasty aroma to this dish that is echoed by the fungic flavour of the mushrooms. If you use a tender cut of meat, such as sirloin, it needs less cooking time than a traditional stew. Serve with jacket potatoes to increase the earthy autumnal feel.

**SERVES 6**

**1 kg organic sirloin steak (trimmed weight)**

**salt and freshly ground black pepper**

**3 tablespoons plain flour**

**7 tablespoons sunflower oil**

**2 onions, finely sliced**

**1 clove garlic, finely diced**

**2 sticks celery, finely sliced**

**3 large carrots, peeled and cut into rounds**

**250 g chestnut mushrooms**

**2 teaspoons Demerara sugar**

**2 tablespoons white wine vinegar**

**250 ml Stella Artois**

**1 bay leaf, plus some parsley and thyme sprigs**

Remove any tough fibres running through the meat before cutting into 5 cm chunks. Season the flour. Heat 3 tablespoons of oil in a large saucepan set over a medium heat. Take a large handful of meat and lightly coat in the seasoned flour, shaking the excess flour back into the bowl, before adding a single layer of meat to the pan.

Fry briskly, turning regularly, for about 3 minutes or until browned on all sides. Transfer the meat to a bowl and colour the remaining steak in batches, adding a little more oil as you need it.

When all the meat has been browned, add a further 2 tablespoons of oil to the pan and lower the heat. Stir in the onions, garlic, celery and carrots and gently fry for 5 minutes or until soft. Increase the heat slightly and mix in the mushrooms, followed by the brown sugar. Cook for 2 minutes, then add the remaining seasoned flour and cook for a further 4 minutes.

Mix in the vinegar, followed by the beer, 300 ml water and the meat with its juices. Bring up to the boil then lower the heat and season to taste. Cover and simmer very gently for 50 minutes. Remove from the heat and allow to sit for 10 minutes before serving so that the juice is reabsorbed into the meat.

## SUGAR PLUM TART

This is not an elegant plum tart that you could serve for tea. Instead it is an overly juicy, messy plumdocious sort of a pudding, where the yeasty smell of the plum-soaked dough evokes drowsy wasps, long shadows and youthful hunger.

**SERVES 8**

**125 ml full fat milk**

**1 teaspoon dried yeast**

**300 g plain flour**

**¼ teaspoon salt**

**50 g caster sugar, plus extra for the plums**

**30 g butter, melted, plus extra for greasing**

**1 medium egg, beaten**

**1 teaspoon cinnamon**

**1.5 kg plums, such as Marjorie Seedling, halved and stoned**

Heat the milk until tepid. Pour into a bowl, sprinkle on the yeast and leave for 10 minutes or until the yeast has dissolved and smells and looks active.

Place the flour, salt and 50 g sugar into a mixing bowl. Stir the cool melted butter into the yeast milk and pour into the flour. Add the beaten egg and, using your hands, mix together until a soft dough forms. Turn out and knead thoroughly for 5–10 minutes or until it feels silky smooth. Return to a bowl, cover and leave to rise in a warm place for an hour.

Butter a 28 cm diameter non-stick baking tart tin with a removable base (about 4 cm deep) or 3 cm deep non-stick baking tray that is 30 x 20 cm. Turn the dough out on to a lightly floured surface. Knock back and roll it out into a round or rectangle large enough to line your buttered baking tray. Trim the edges of the rim if necessary. Prick the base with a fork.

Preheat the oven to Gas Mark 7/220°C. Mix 4 tablespoons of caster sugar with the cinnamon and toss the plums in the spiced sugar. Arrange them standing up at a slight angle on the dough so that they come up to the rim and are tightly packed. Leave to rise for 30 minutes.

Bake in the oven for 20–25 minutes or until the dough is golden brown and the plums are cooked. Remove from the oven and sprinkle with a further 4 tablespoons caster sugar. Don't worry if the plums are swimming in juice, this soaks into the crust to make a luscious soft yeasty plum pudding. It is best eaten warm or cold.

# OCTOBER TOAST

## A SLICE OF TOAST IN THE MORNING

As the year slips into autumn, different scents appear. Outside, the cold air smells of hoar frost on long grass and fluttering yellow leaves. Inside, the smell of freshly ground coffee and buttered toast fill the warm kitchen before curling up through the house. It is time to shake off summer's fragrance and play with the darker, richer flavours of autumn.

Toast aromas are very closely associated with bitter tastes as they are created at the moment before something burns.

Bitterness is an adult taste as it often indicates that a food will disturb our metabolism. Caffeine, nicotine and strychnine, for example, all taste bitter. As a result, babies and young children find bitter tastes repulsive, no doubt as a protective measure, and will only slowly develop a taste for them as they grow older. Consequently, toast aromas tend to be associated with that bubbling warm excitement you feel as you are growing up and experiencing more of life, regardless of whether it is eating piles of buttered toast as a teenager or sampling your first bitter sweet salted caramel at the end of an expensive meal.

Creating toast flavours in food relies on utilising certain culinary techniques, for example, caramelising sugar, browning butter or roasting coffee beans. It is a complex category of smell, closely bound to other similar flavour groups such as nut, caramel and savoury. Think of the myriad notes to be found in the smell of fried onions wafting on the cold autumn air from a hot dog stall.

Harold McGee in his book, *McGee on Food & Cooking, An Encyclopedia of Kitchen Science, History and Culture* (2004), explains that when food turns brown as a result of being subjected to heat, a chemical reaction occurs in which the molecular structure of the food changes, which in turn creates new tastes and flavours. Thus, a warm golden-topped bread and butter pudding has an alluring toasty smell as a result of the chemical reaction it has undergone in the oven.

From the cook's perspective, adding a toast note to a dish is likely to produce positive reactions in the eater; that tummy tingling feeling of youthful excitement mixed with comforting familiarity, such as when you suddenly catch the scent of freshly cooked praline drifting down a French street or the irresistible smell of fried bread and tomatoes wafting from an English café as you walk to work. This subliminal reaction can be used to great effect when entertaining.

# SESAME PRAWN TOASTS

October, to my mind, marks the beginning of party time. Dark nights, bright lights and cooks racking their brains for some new canapés. Naturally, if you add a toast flavour to nibbles, such as here, it should, in theory at least, instil a feeling of teenage excitement in your guests.

**MAKES 30**

**corn oil for deep frying**

**10 slices stale white bread**

**1 bunch spring onions, trimmed**

**450 g raw prawns, shelled and roughly chopped**

**100 g minced pork**

**1 teaspoon salt**

**1 medium egg white**

**1 1/2 teaspoons finely chopped ginger**

**1 tablespoon Kikkoman soy sauce**

**2 teaspoons toasted sesame oil**

**2 teaspoons caster sugar**

**3 tablespoons sesame seeds**

Preheat the oven to Gas Mark 1/2 /120°C. Half fill a deep fat fryer or one third fill a large pan with the oil. If using a pan, clip on a thermometer. Heat the oil to 180°C.

Remove the crusts from the bread and cut each slice into three pieces about 7.5 x 2.5 cm. Place them in the oven for 5 minutes so that they toast lightly without colouring.

Meanwhile, roughly slice the white parts of the spring onions and place in a food processor with the prawns, pork, salt, egg white, ginger, soy sauce, sesame oil and sugar. Whiz in short bursts to form a rough paste.

Spread the prawn paste thickly over each piece of toast and sprinkle with the sesame seeds. Drop the prawn toasts, paste side down, into the hot oil a few at a time and fry for 2 minutes. Then flip them over and fry for another 2 minutes until golden brown. Remove and drain on kitchen paper. Repeat until all the toasts are cooked.

## MELBA TOAST

The ultimate toasty flavour can be conjured up by serving Melba toast. This can be prepared a day or two ahead and stored in an airtight container. It's delicious served with the Buttered prawns (see page 63) or the Kipper paste (see page 28).

**SERVES 6**

**12 slices white bread**

Preheat the oven to Gas Mark 2/150°C. Lightly toast the sliced bread in the toaster. Cut off the crusts and gently split the bread in half horizontally. Arrange the toast on a couple of baking sheets, uncooked side up, and place in the preheated oven. Bake until golden brown and crisp.

# CARAMELISED ONION SOUP

Caramelised onions can taste very sweet and cloying in onion soup. However, because in this recipe they are initially cooked in wine, they have a fresher flavour that allows through the subtle toast notes that can be found in the toasted croûtons, caramelised onions and grilled cheese. It evokes for many memories of student life, creating a feeling of comfort mixed with a sense of new beginnings.

**SERVES 4**

**500 g onions, finely sliced**

**1 clove garlic, finely sliced**

**500 ml dry white wine**

**55 g butter**

**1 litre good chicken stock (see page 168)**

**salt and freshly ground black pepper**

**8 slices sourdough baguette**

**55 g finely grated French Emmental**

Preheat the oven to Gas Mark 7/220°C. Place the onions, garlic, wine and butter in an ovenproof saucepan. Mix together and place in the preheated oven. Cook for an hour, stirring often to prevent the exposed onions from burning.

Once the wine has almost evaporated, transfer the pan to the hob and set over a low heat. Stir the onions regularly until they turn soft and golden brown and the wine has evaporated. This second stage will take about 35 minutes.

Add the stock, bring up to the boil and season to taste. If wished, the soup can be chilled or frozen at this point.

Shortly before serving, preheat the grill to high. Reheat the onion soup and simmer for 5–10 minutes. Lightly toast the slices of bread. Cover each piece of bread with some of the grated cheese, place under the grill and watch closely. Remove as soon as the cheese has melted and is beginning to turn golden. Divide the soup between four soup bowls, place two cheesy croûtons on each bowl and serve immediately.

## SOLE WITH BEURRE NOISETTE

The flavour of melted butter can be deepened by gently browning it to a golden brown. This creates a nutty toasted flavour. If the butter is cooked until it is a darker brown it takes on a more caramelised flavour. The latter is known as black butter or beurre noir.

Fish is most succulent cooked on the bone but, if you don't like tackling bones, you can ask the fishmonger to fillet the fish. Try serving with Chips (see page 133).

**SERVES 2**

**85 g unsalted butter**

**2 x 450 g Dover sole, skinned**

**2 tablespoons plain flour**

**salt and freshly ground black pepper**

**½ lemon, cut into wedges**

To make the clarified butter, place 55 g butter in a small saucepan. Set over a low heat and gently simmer for 8–10 minutes or until the melted butter throws up a thick white froth. Strain through a very fine sieve, or a sieve lined with damp muslin, into a small bowl, discarding the froth and any milky liquid in the bottom of the saucepan as you do so. Clarified butter can be cooked at a higher temperature than normal melted butter. Set aside until needed.

Cut off the heads of the fish and, using kitchen scissors, cut away the fan-like fins that run down each side. Snip off the tails. Place the flour in a large bowl and season.

Set a frying pan over a medium heat. Once hot, add the clarified butter. Quickly dip each fish into the flour and shake off the excess. Immediately add the fish to the sizzling hot butter and fry for about 4 minutes on each side until golden brown and cooked through. Remove to warm plates.

Place 30 g cold butter in a small saucepan. Set over a medium heat until it turns golden brown and smells of hazelnuts. Immediately pour over the fish. Garnish with lemon wedges and serve immediately.

## BREADCRUMBED CHICKEN

One of the easiest ways to add a toast flavour to food is to coat it in breadcrumbs and fry it. Adding mustard creates a wonderful bite. In summer, I add chopped herbs, such as tarragon, chives and parsley, to the mustard cream and serve the chicken cold for a picnic lunch.

This recipe can also be adapted to white fish, veal or pork.

**SERVES 4**

**150 g soft white breadcrumbs**

**2 tablespoons smooth Dijon mustard**

**½ tablespoon English mustard powder**

**140 ml double cream**

**salt and freshly ground black pepper**

**2 tablespoons plain flour**

**4 skinned, organic chicken breasts, each about 150 g**

**sunflower or corn oil**

Prepare the breadcrumbs by cutting off the crusts from slices of stale white bread and whizzing the bread in a food processor. Place 150 g of crumbs in a shallow bowl and set aside. Breadcrumbs freeze well, so make them whenever you have excess bread.

Mix together the mustard, mustard powder and cream in a bowl large enough to hold the chicken pieces. Season to taste. Place the flour in a third bowl and season. Set out a tray or two plates for the breadcrumbed chicken.

Trim the chicken breasts of any sinews or fat. Remove the underlying fillets and slice each breast into three or four pieces. Dust all the chicken pieces, including the fillets, in the flour, shaking off the excess before mixing into the mustard cream. Finally, coat each piece in the breadcrumbs, firmly pressing them into the cream. Lay on the tray or plates. Once all are coated, lightly cover with cling film and chill until you are ready to cook.

Set two non-stick frying pans over a medium heat. Add 4 tablespoons oil to each pan and, once sizzling hot, add a single layer of crumbed chicken to each pan. Cook for about 4 minutes on each side or until golden and cooked through. Drain on kitchen paper. If necessary, wipe out one of the pans, add more oil and fry the remaining chicken. Serve hot, warm or cold.

# CHIPS

I can't resist the toasty yet fragrant potato flavour of chips! They are one of my favourite foods, hence the recipe here. In fact potatoes can be used to create a number of toast flavours ranging from crisps to the caramelised top of a potato gratin. Since I love thin 'French fry' style of chips, my recipe is for thin chips. If you're a chunky chip person, follow the same method but allow longer cooking times for your thicker cut chips. If you want to serve them in cones, as shown in the photograph on page 131, make a little inner cone of greaseproof paper to protect the chips from the newspaper print.

**SERVES 4**
**4 large potatoes, preferably King Edwards**
**corn oil for deep frying**
**salt**

Peel the potatoes and cut into thin chip-sized batons. Place in a large bowl of cold water and leave to soak for 30 minutes to remove the excess starch.

Preheat the oil in a deep fat fryer to 150°C. If you don't have a deep fat fryer, pour enough oil to reach a third of the way up the side of a large heavy-bottomed saucepan and clip on a thermometer.

Drain the chipped potatoes and pat dry on some paper towelling. Cook in batches so that the oil retains its temperature as the potatoes 'blanch'. Fry the potatoes until they have a crisp uncoloured skin with a soft centre. This will take around 4 minutes. Remove from the oil and shake off the excess before spreading them out to cool on some kitchen paper. Once cold, either set aside or, if you're prepping well ahead, chill until shortly before needed. The blanched chips should be at room temperature before the final cooking.

To serve, heat the oil to 180°C and cook the blanched chips in batches for about 3 minutes or until golden and crisp. Drain on kitchen paper, tip into a mixing bowl and salt liberally before dropping a pile of chips on to each plate.

## PEAR CRÈME CARAMEL

In a larger book on flavour, caramel would have its own chapter (along with nut) but, given caramel's closeness to toast aromas, I've slipped it in here instead.

This recipe is very creamy; for a lighter texture, use 100 ml milk and 150 ml cream.

**SERVES 6**

**3 ripe medium-sized pears, peeled, cored, quartered and roughly chopped**
**50 ml full fat milk**
**200 ml double cream**
**1 vanilla pod, split**
**2 medium eggs**
**4 medium egg yolks**
**100 g caster sugar**
**150 g granulated sugar**

Place the pears in a saucepan with 1 tablespoon water. Cover and set over a medium-low heat. Simmer for 15 minutes or until the pears are meltingly soft. Purée and measure out 250 ml.

Meanwhile, put the milk, cream and vanilla pod in a saucepan. Bring up to boiling point, remove from the heat, cover and leave to infuse for 20 minutes. Remove the vanilla pod.

Put the eggs and egg yolks in a bowl with the caster sugar. Whisk lightly and mix in the vanilla milk and 250 ml pear purée. Strain the mixture into a jug, cover and chill for 2 hours, giving it the odd stir if the mixture separates slightly. It will thicken as it cools.

Preheat the oven to Gas Mark 2/150°C. Place the granulated sugar in a heavy-based saucepan with 150 ml boiling water. Set over a low heat and stir occasionally until the sugar has dissolved. Boil until it is a rich golden caramel colour, then divide between six 150 ml ramekins. Work quickly as the caramel will continue to darken as you pour.

Arrange the ramekins in a roasting tray. Skim any froth from the custard and pour into the ramekins. Add cold water to the tray to come two-thirds of the way up the side of the dishes. Bake for 40 minutes or until just set. The custards should wobble but not ripple. Chill for at least 6 hours.

To serve, loosen the edges of each custard with a knife, then place a rimmed plate over the top of each crème caramel and invert it so that the custard slips out with its caramel sauce.

## SALTED SCOTTISH TABLET

The scent of bubbling butter, milk and sugar as it starts to caramelise and turn into fudge reawakens the childish pleasure to be found in creating something out of nothing. This has a grown-up twist with its salty flavour.

**MAKES 525 G OR ABOUT 42 LARGE PIECES**

**55 g unsalted butter, plus extra for greasing**

**450 g granulated sugar**

**255 ml creamy milk**

**1 tablespoon golden syrup**

**1 teaspoon sea salt**

**1 teaspoon vanilla extract**

Grease a 20 cm-square and 2.5 cm-deep tray with butter. Set aside.

Clip a thermometer onto a heavy-bottomed saucepan and add the sugar, butter, milk, syrup and salt. Place over a moderate heat and stir until the ingredients have dissolved. Bring slowly to the boil and boil hard until the mixture reaches 116°C (soft ball stage).

Remove from the heat immediately, add the vanilla extract and beat vigorously with a wooden spoon or wooden spatula until the mixture changes its consistency and becomes thick, pale and creamy. This gives it a melt in the mouth texture but will take a good 5–10 minutes. Quickly pour into the greased tray before the mixture becomes too firm and leave to cool.

Cut the fudge into squares as soon as it begins to set – it will be impossible to break into pieces later. Eat when hard. As the fudge melts in your mouth, myriad complex toast notes are released.

## TOASTED TEA CAKES

The scent of hot tea mixed with the smoky smell of an open fire adds an indefinable dimension to buttered crumpets, anchovy toast and toasted tea cakes. Few can resist an old-fashioned tea on a rain-lashed October afternoon. These cakes are best toasted the day after baking, but they also taste good in a spicy untoasty way when eaten freshly baked.

**MAKES 8**

**285 ml full fat milk**

**2 teaspoons dried yeast**

**500 g plain flour**

**1 teaspoon salt**

**1 teaspoon mixed spice**

**55 g chilled unsalted butter, diced**

**45 g caster sugar**

**115 g currants**

**1 medium egg**

**For the glaze:**

**4 tablespoons milk**

**3 tablespoons caster sugar**

Heat the milk until tepid, pour into a jug and sprinkle the yeast on the top. Leave for at least 10 minutes or until the yeast has dissolved and looks active.

Meanwhile, place the flour in a food processor with the salt and mixed spice. Briefly whiz then add the diced butter and process until it forms fine breadcrumbs. If you do not have a food processor, rub the butter in with your fingertips. Tip into a large mixing bowl and mix in the sugar followed by the currants. Add the yeasty milk. Beat the egg in the same jug as the milk and add to the flour. Mix thoroughly. The dough will be very soft and quite sticky.

Turn the dough out on to a clean surface and knead by stretching and folding the dough under the palm of one hand until smooth and silky. This will take about 5 minutes. Place in a clean bowl, cover and leave to rise for an hour or until doubled in size.

Preheat the oven to Gas Mark 6/200°C. Divide the dough into eight even-sized pieces. Shape each piece into a round roll, place on two non-stick baking sheets and flatten each roll into a 10-cm diameter disc. Prick the discs with a fork and cover each tray with a clean tea towel. Leave for 40 minutes or until the discs look puffy.

Bake in the oven for 15–20 minutes or until well risen and golden. Meanwhile, prepare the glaze by heating the milk and sugar in a small pan until the sugar has dissolved, then boil for 1 minute until syrupy. As soon as the tea cakes are cooked, tip on to a cooling rack. Brush with the warm glaze while they are hot.

The buns can be split open and liberally buttered while warm. However, if you want to savour a toasty flavour, save half for the next day and eat toasted. Split open, toast under the grill and spread with lots of butter.

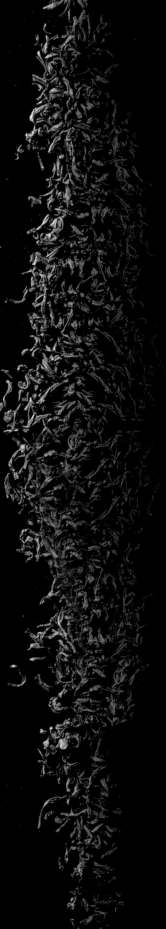

## WOOD SMOKE CURLING INTO THE COLD NIGHT AIR

It is easy to become addicted to the subtle complexity of smoky flavours: they add an indefinable quality to dishes that can make them irresistible. This may be partly due to the fact that many smoked foods are rich in umami, which makes them taste doubly delicious, but I suspect that smokiness also hints at something mysterious and ethereal, which adds to the food's allure. Consequently, a wise cook will always use smoky flavours with a light hand to ensure that their diners are intrigued rather than overwhelmed by such notes.

Smoke flavours are the equivalent of mid-notes in perfumery. They tend to be the dominant flavour in a given food such as sticky barbecued ribs or smoked trout. Top notes, such as citrus zest, are instantly perceived but quickly fade, while bottom notes, such as cloves, are slow to develop and linger in the mouth long after the top notes have faded.

Your use of smoky flavours will vary according to your environment. In Northern India, for example, the evening air hangs heavy with smoke from small fires fuelled by dried cow pats. Their intense aroma, mixed with spices and sizzling ghee, permeates the Indian cook's perception of life. Adding smoky flavourings such as tar-like black cardamoms or heavy-scented cloves to aromatic rice and dahl dishes creates a pleasing resonance with the smell of everyday life. The British cook, meanwhile, draws on a different array of familiar smells such as autumn fogs, peat fires, freshly brewed tea and garden bonfires. These aromas are captured in smoked salmon, Islay malt whisky, Lapsang Souchong tea and smoky bacon.

Use everyday scents as a source of inspiration when you're trying to devise new recipes. This might be the dreamy smell of peat smoke, heather and sea spray in the Outer Hebrides, or wood smoke on a cold November London night mixed with a hint of Indian restaurant cooking and taxi cab fumes. The former might find expression in a simple Kipper paste (see page 28) with Oat cakes (see page 44), while the latter might be translated into brightly coloured Chilli beans, flavoured with the deep tones of smoked Spanish paprika (see page 144).

## SMOKED SALMON, GRILLED LEEK AND FENNEL SALAD

One way to introduce smoke flavours to food during the winter is to replace the summer barbecue with an oven-top cast-iron griddle pan. As the food sears, it takes on a smoky flavour. This dish typifies London-meets-the-countryside to me.

**SERVES 4**

**24 baby leeks**

**1 plump Florence fennel**

**6 tablespoons extra virgin olive oil**

**2 tablespoons salted capers**

**1½ tablespoons white wine vinegar**

**salt and freshly ground black pepper**

**the heart of a leafy chicory or curly endive**

**275 g smoked salmon, finely sliced**

Preheat an oven-top griddle pan over a medium-high heat. Trim the leeks, cutting away their roots and their dark green leaves. Remove the tough outer leaves and cut a cross in the pale green sections – to create a mop-like look. Wash them thoroughly in cold water. Trim the fennel, removing any scarred outer layers, cut in half and slice each half into fans.

Bring a large pan of unsalted water to the boil and add the leeks. Return to the boil and cook briskly for 2 minutes or until the leeks are al dente. Remove and spread out to cool. Meanwhile, add the sliced fennel to the boiling water. Return to the boil and cook for a brief minute, then drain and spread out to cool.

Once cool, dry the leeks and fennel with kitchen paper and place in a bowl. Coat in 2 tablespoons of olive oil then place a single layer of oiled leeks on the preheated griddle pan. As soon as they are flecked golden, turn over and colour the other side. Remove to a plate and leave to cool while you continue to grill the remaining leeks. Repeat the process with the fennel.

Rinse the capers and pat dry on kitchen paper. In a large bowl whisk together the vinegar and 4 tablespoons olive oil. Add the capers and season to taste. Set aside until needed. Wash and dry the salad leaves. You only need enough to add a little body to the salad.

When you are ready to serve, mix the leeks, fennel and salad leaves into the vinaigrette. Divide into airy piles between four plates. Rip the smoked salmon into wide strips and carefully tuck waves of smoked salmon in amongst the salad. Serve immediately.

## MUSHROOMS, SMOKED HAM AND CHEESE ON TOAST

Smoked foods, such as ham, can add a pensive, wintery note. This dish also illustrates the benefits of combining smoked food with fungic and toast flavours.

**SERVES 2**

**2 thick slices sourdough bread**

**1 tablespoon extra virgin olive oil**

**1 small clove garlic, finely chopped**

**185 g button mushrooms, trimmed and halved**

**15 g unsalted butter**

**salt and freshly ground black pepper**

**1 tablespoon lemon juice**

**4 fine slices smoked lean ham**

**50 g French Emmental cheese, finely sliced**

Preheat the oven grill to high and set an oven-top griddle pan over a moderate heat. Line the grill pan with foil and have it close to hand. When everything is ready, place the bread on the griddle pan and toast for 1½ minutes on each side or until lightly toasted and marked with griddle lines. Set on the grill rack, but not under the heat.

Meanwhile, set a small frying pan over a medium heat. Add the olive oil and garlic. As soon as the garlic begins to sizzle, add the mushrooms and butter and season to taste. Stir fry briskly for 2 minutes, or until the mushrooms are lightly cooked, then add the lemon juice. Remove from the heat and spoon the mushrooms on to the toast. Divide the juices equally and heap the mushrooms up.

Rip the ham into strips, discarding any fat as you do so, and gently place on top of the mushrooms, tucking it in slightly if necessary. Top with the sliced cheese and place under the grill. Cook for about 5 minutes or until the cheese is bubbling and golden. Serve immediately.

# SMOKED HADDOCK KEDGEREE

This unusual kedgeree has the merest pinch of spice and provides a very British perception of flavour. The hint of smokiness from the smoked haddock conjures up Scotland with its wild seas, crofts and small farms. I normally serve this recipe for supper, but it also makes an enjoyable light lunch.

**SERVES 4**

**4 medium eggs, at room temperature**

**2 x 300 g smoked haddock fillets**

**1 bay leaf**

**8 scallops, cleaned and quartered**

**½ teaspoon cayenne pepper**

**salt and freshly ground black pepper**

**55 g unsalted butter**

**225 g button mushrooms, quartered**

**juice of 1 lemon**

**284 ml double cream**

**200 g peeled, cooked North Atlantic
   prawns**

**6 tablespoons finely chopped parsley**

**basmati rice to serve**

Place the eggs in a small saucepan of cold water. Gently bring up to the boil and simmer for 10 minutes until hard boiled. Drain and cool under cold water.

Meanwhile, put the haddock fillets in a saucepan with the bay leaf and cover with cold water. Set over a medium heat, bring up to the boil and simmer for 5 minutes or until the haddock is just cooked. The flesh should flake away from the skin. Drain and,

once cool, remove the flesh in large flakes and place in a clean saucepan, ensuring that there are no remaining bones or skin.

Set a non-stick frying pan over a high heat. Toss the scallops in the cayenne pepper and lightly season with salt and freshly ground black pepper. Add half the butter to the hot pan, swirl quickly and add the scallops. Stir fry briskly for a couple of minutes until seared but tender, then transfer the scallops to the pan containing the flaked haddock. Add the remaining butter to the pan and stir in the mushrooms. Lightly season and fry briskly over a medium heat for 3 minutes or until just cooked. Add 2 tablespoons lemon juice and tip into the haddock.

Peel, halve and roughly chop the eggs. Mix into the haddock along with the cream. Squeeze any excess water from the prawns and mix in. The kedgeree can be covered and chilled at this stage if wished.

When you are ready to serve, set over a low heat and stir frequently until hot. Don't boil or you will over-cook it and the prawns and scallops will become tough. Adjust the seasoning to taste, adding another 2 tablespoons lemon juice and a pinch of cayenne pepper if necessary. Stir in the parsley and serve with plenty of basmati rice. (See page 159 for quantities and method for the rice. To cook plainly, omit the saffron and shallots.)

## CHILLI BEANS, AVOCADO AND SOUR CREAM

Smoke flavours come in many different forms, but one of the most alluring is smoked sweet Spanish paprika. It has a warm, rich, smoky note that enhances stews and pulses. It's worth making large quantites of this chilli as it freezes well, in which case use green, orange and red peppers.

If you want to cook your own beans, soak 200 g black beans in plenty of cold water overnight. Drain, rinse and place in a large saucepan with a halved onion, clove of garlic, celery stick, bay leaf and coriander stalks. Cover with cold water, boil vigorously for 10 minutes, then simmer for about an hour or until soft. Drain and cook as described below.

---

**SERVES 4**

**3 tablespoons extra virgin olive oil**

**1 onion, finely diced**

**1 clove garlic, finely diced**

**1 Thai chilli (or to taste), finely diced**

**2 sticks celery, finely diced**

**1 green pepper, deseeded
    and finely diced**

**½ teaspoon cumin seeds**

**1 teaspoon smoked paprika**

**1 sprig fresh oregano**

**2 sprigs lemon thyme**

**1 bay leaf**

**2 strips finely pared lemon zest**

**400 g can chopped tomatoes**

**2 x 410 g cans black beans,
    drained and rinsed**

**salt and freshly ground black pepper**

**To serve:**

**2 ripe avocados**

**2 tablespoons lemon juice**

**4 tablespoons soured cream**

**a large handful coriander leaves**

Set a large pan over medium-low heat. Add the oil and, once hot, add the onion, garlic, chilli, celery and green pepper. Fry for 8 minutes or until the vegetables are soft and golden. Mix in the cumin seeds and paprika. Fry for a further minute then mix in the herbs, lemon zest, canned tomatoes and rinsed beans. Half fill one of the tomato tins with water, stir into the mixture and bring to the boil. Season the chili beans to taste and simmer for 30 minutes.

Meanwhile, quarter, stone and peel the avocados. Cut into slices and toss in the lemon juice. Season to taste. When you are ready to serve, divide the beans between four plates and top each portion with avocado and a spoonful of soured cream. Scatter with coriander leaves and serve immediately.

# WHISKY RUM BABA

**MAKES 10**

**200 g sultanas**
**450 ml Islay whisky, such as Laphroaig**
**2 teaspoons dried yeast**
**250 g plain flour**
**½ teaspoon salt**
**3½ organic lemons**
**2 tablespoons honey**
**5 medium eggs**
**100 g very soft butter, plus extra**
**450 g unrefined granulated sugar**
**300 g crème fraîche**
**2 tablespoons icing sugar, or to taste**
**5 peeled bananas, cut into half moons**

You will need 10 x 150 ml dariole moulds for this recipe. Soak the sultanas in 450 ml whisky overnight. The next day, drain the sultanas, saving the whisky. Set aside half the fruit in a bowl. Sprinkle the yeast into 2 tablespoons tepid water in a small bowl. Leave for 10 minutes or until the yeast has dissolved and looks active.

Mix the flour, salt and finely grated zest of 1 lemon in a bowl. Tip into your food processor. Gently melt the honey in a small pan. Pour into a bowl and beat in 3 eggs. Add the egg mixture to the flour. Add the yeast and beat thoroughly with the dough hook. Add the butter and beat until the dough looks smooth, then add a further 2 eggs, one at a time, beating thoroughly until you have an elastic dough. Beat in half the sultanas. Scrape the dough into a bowl,

cover and leave to rise in a warm place for 2 hours or until doubled in size.

Preheat the oven to Gas Mark 5/190°C. Butter the moulds. Flour your hands and divide the dough equally between each mould. Press each piece of dough down with a floured teaspoon. The moulds should be about half full. Cover them with a clean cloth and leave for 30 minutes or until the dough has risen to three-quarters fill the tins.

Meanwhile, make the syrup by placing the 450 g sugar in a saucepan with 450 ml water and the finely pared zest of 2½ lemons. Set over a medium heat. Once the sugar has dissolved, boil briskly for 10 minutes. Add the juice of 2½ lemons and 115 ml of the sultana whisky. Strain into a bowl and pour a little into the remaining sultanas.

Remove the cloth and place the moulds on a baking tray. Bake for 15–20 minutes or until they are golden and springy. Turn out on to a wire rack. Pierce each baba all over with a fine skewer and, while warm, dip into the syrup before returning to its mould. Strain the syrup into a jug and pour over each baba until well soaked.

Whisk the crème fraîche, 50 ml of the sultana whisky and the icing sugar until thick. Mix the sliced bananas with the remaining sultanas. Toss in some of the syrup. When you are ready to serve, turn out the rum babas, glaze with any extra syrup and serve with the bananas and whisky cream.

# DECEMBER SPICE

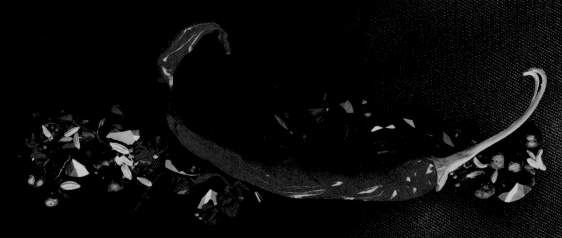

# CINNAMON ROLLS WARM FROM THE OVEN

Spicy flavours capture the emotion and excitement of cooking. A pinch of this, a few blades of that, and a dish can be transformed into something exotic or homely depending on the whim of the cook. The breadth of spice flavour is extraordinary; it can range from liquorice-like star anise and musky cloves to the fresh tingle of Sichuan peppercorns and the faint citrus heat of mace

Some cooks, and I would count my husband among these, love to see spices as part of their culinary laboratory. They are laid out and their flavours mentally analysed and combined in relation to the dish in progress. Other cooks, such as myself, tend to treat spices like paint, mixing instinctively, rather than rationally, to evoke a mood or memory. Every spice has its associations. The peppery-like smell of allspice, for example, is linked in my memory with my early struggles as a cook – chill damp winter days in tense restaurant kitchens and the longed for, other-worldliness of Elizabeth David's recipes in *Spices, Salt and Aromatics in the English Kitchen* (1970), where allspice was used to flavour pickles, Christmas pudding and terrine.

The scents of all spices instantly provoke an emotional reaction. Cinnamon, for example, is much loved by perfumery companies, who create cinnamon-scented Christmas candles to imbue households with a warm, festive glow. Vanilla, on the other hand, is used to calm frayed nerves. However, it's better by far to bake some sticky cinnamon rolls or wave some mulled wine under the noses of difficult guests. They will instantly melt as they munch or sip your tempting offerings.

Choosing spices for a recipe can be key to bringing out the integral flavour of your chosen ingredients. As Tom Stobart wrote in *Herbs, Spices and Flavourings* (1970), 'Very often the secrets of the great chefs have been tiny amounts of unusual flavouring added in unrecognizable quantities. To do this requires not only imagination, but a good knowledge of the possibilities.' Therein lie two of the great pleasures of cooking – exploration and creation. The exquisite yet unexpected combination of green cardamom seeds in a warm pear tart tatin lingers long in the memory after the dish has been eaten.

In December I tend to draw on a palette of warm-flavoured spices such as cloves, cumin, black pepper, vanilla, allspice and cinnamon. Their smell conjures up the romance of the Christmas holidays, when splattered old cook books are put to work in a bustling kitchen, deep in preparation for a week of festive eating. However, when you are scanning your spices, it is worth remembering that part of the allure of many spices is that they contain pungent chemicals that literally irritate the eater's mouth. Capsaiscin in chilli, piperine in black pepper and shogal in dried ginger are just a few examples. It is these tasteless, flavourless chemicals that literally excite the eater and add an extra dimension to food.

## GAME TERRINE

A good meat or game terrine requires sensitive spicing to lighten its essentially meaty flavour. Traditionally, mace, nutmeg, allspice, cloves, juniper berries or quatre-épices (a mixture of pepper, nutmeg, cloves and either cinnamon or ginger) can be used.

You will need a 600 g capacity rectangular porcelain terrine mould with a lid for this recipe. In *Roast Chicken and Other Stories* (1994) Simon Hopkinson recommends manually chopping the meat for a terrine as this gives the best texture. He's right, and it's not as hard as it sounds. This tastes best eaten a day or two after cooking.

---

**SERVES 8**
**200 g skinned pheasant breasts**
**175 g skinned partridge breasts**
**115 g pork back fat**
**6 slices streaky bacon**
**55 g unsalted butter**
**1 onion, finely diced**
**1 clove garlic, finely diced**
**1 medium egg**
**2 tablespoons fresh breadcrumbs**
**2 tablespoons Rémy Martin cognac**
**⅛ teaspoon ground allspice**
**a pinch of freshly grated nutmeg**
**½ teaspoon herbes de Provence**
**salt and freshly ground black pepper**

Preheat the oven to Gas Mark 3/170°C. If necessary, skin the pheasant and partridge breasts. Remove any sinews and finely dice. Finely dice the back fat and bacon. Mix all the meat together, then place in a centre of a large board and, using a large chef's knife, chop finely. This mixes the meat as it is minced. Tip into a mixing bowl.

Melt the butter in a frying pan set over a low heat. Add the onion and garlic and fry gently for 5 minutes or until soft and golden. Mix the softened onions into the minced meat with the egg, breadcrumbs, cognac, spices, herbs and seasoning. Beat thoroughly and check the seasoning by frying off a small patty of meat.

Place all the meat into the terrine, pressing firmly and evenly. Cover with a small sheet of buttered paper then cover with the lid. Place in a roasting tray. Add enough boiling water to come half way up the side of the terrine and bake for an hour. The terrine is cooked when the meat has shrunk away from the edges and the juices run clear.

Remove from the roasting tray. Remove the lid. Add a further sheet of paper and place a heavy weight on top. Leave to cool. Once cold, remove the weight, cover and chill. Serve sliced with buttered toast and gherkins.

## SPICED ROAST PEPPERS WITH MOZZARELLA

In the depths of winter, the cook's art lies in combining evocative spices with rich colours and intense tastes. This appetizer is by nature sweet and sour, deeply coloured and satisfyingly spicy.

**SERVES 6**

**6 peppers (a mixture of red, yellow and orange)**

**6 tablespoons extra virgin olive oil**

**1 clove garlic, finely diced**

**1 teaspoon cumin seeds**

**1 teaspoon chilli flakes**

**40 g raisins**

**30 g flaked almonds**

**15 g caster sugar**

**3 tablespoons white wine vinegar**

**salt and freshly ground black pepper**

**4 tablespoons finely chopped parsley leaves**

**3 balls buffalo mozzarella**

Preheat the grill to high. Quarter and core the peppers. Place skin-side up under the hot grill and cook until the skin blisters and blackens. Remove to a bowl and cover. Once cool, peel off the skin and cut the flesh lengthwise into medium-thick strips.

Set a wide saucepan over a medium heat. Add the olive oil and, when hot, mix in the roasted pepper strips. Once they're hot, stir in the garlic, cumin seeds, chilli flakes, raisins, almonds and sugar. Fry for 2 minutes, stirring regularly. Mix in the vinegar once the ingredients begin to cook but before the almonds turn brown. Bubble vigorously until the vinegar has evaporated. Remove from the heat, season to taste and leave until tepid. Mix in the parsley.

Slice the mozzarella and divide between six plates. Spoon on the peppers so that they partially fall on to the cheese. Serve immediately.

## FRAGRANT LAMB CURRY

If there is one style of dish dependent on a sensitive marriage of spice, it is the curry. Use Indian spices where possible, such as the Rajah brand. Don't use smoked paprika. This dish is also good made with Kashmiri chillies instead of normal Indian chilli powder. They have a milder heat, so grind and experiment with the quantity.

This tastes better the next day. Half a teaspoon of normal chilli powder makes a mild curry. Try serving with Saffron rice cooked with peas (see opposite).

**SERVES 6**

**900 g boneless lamb loin fillets, cut into 2 cm chunks**

**2 teaspoons paprika**

**5 tablespoons sunflower oil**

**a large pinch of saffron threads**

**salt**

**10 green cardamoms**

**½ teaspoon ground turmeric**

**½ –1 teaspoon Indian chilli powder, or to taste**

**300 g shallots, finely sliced**

**1 tablespoon finely shredded, peeled ginger**

**4 cloves**

**100 ml thick Greek yoghurt**

**200 g baby new potatoes, halved or quartered**

Mix the diced lamb with the paprika and 2 tablespoons sunflower oil. Set aside.

Grind the saffron threads under a teaspoon with a pinch of salt and dissolve in 200 ml warm water. Set aside. Remove the black seeds from the cardamoms. Grind under a rolling pin or with a mortar and pestle. Mix the cardamon powder with the turmeric and chilli powder,

Place a heavy saucepan over a medium heat. Add 3 tablespoons oil and, once hot, stir in the shallots and ginger. Fry briskly, stirring regularly, for 6 minutes or until golden brown. Add the cloves and the ground spice mix. Fry for 2 minutes, then increase the heat to high and mix in the diced lamb. Stir briskly until the meat is well coloured. Add the saffron water, yoghurt and potatoes. Season to taste and bring up to the boil, then reduce the heat to low, cover and simmer gently for 30–40 minutes or until the meat is tender and the potatoes are cooked. Remove from the heat and leave to sit for 20 minutes before serving. This allows the juices to return to the meat.

## SAFFRON RICE

If you are making this to accompany the Fragrant lamb curry opposite, add frozen petit pois after you've fried the rice and continue as described below. Although I've given the weight of the rice below, the easiest way to cook basmati rice is to allow ½ cup rice for two people or 1 cup if you have hearty appetites. Then simple double the quantity of water, in other words, 1 or 2 cups depending on your portion size. For six people, treble all the quantities.

**SERVES 2**
**a pinch of saffron threads**
**a pinch of salt**
**1 tablespoon extra virgin olive oil**
**1 shallot, finely sliced**
**135 g basmati rice**
**30 g frozen petit pois (optional)**
**1 bay leaf (optional)**

Place the saffron threads in a small bowl with a pinch of salt and grind to a powder with the back of a teaspoon. Add 300 ml hot water and leave to infuse.

Set a saucepan over a low heat. Add the oil and, once hot, gently fry the sliced shallot for 3 minutes or until soft and golden. Stir in the rice and cook for a further minute or until it looks slightly translucent. If cooking with peas, add them now. Add the bay leaf and saffron water. Cover and turn the heat to high. As soon as the rice boils, reduce the heat to its lowest setting and leave to simmer for 12–15 minutes or until the water is absorbed. Turn off the heat and leave covered for 10 minutes. The rice is ready when it is fluffy and just past al dente.

## SAFFRON PRAWN SPAGHETTI

Saffron is the lapis lazuli of the spice world. Costly yet desirable, it is most effective when combined with the simplest of fine ingredients, such as here.

**SERVES 2**

**a pinch of saffron threads**

**salt**

**1 tablespoon white wine vinegar**

**225 g ripe tomatoes**

**5 tablespoons extra virgin olive oil**

**1 tablespoon finely sliced basil leaves**

**freshly ground black pepper**

**12 whole raw tiger prawns**

**185 g spaghetti**

**1 clove garlic, finely chopped**

**½ teaspoon dried chilli flakes (optional)**

Place the saffron in a small bowl with a pinch of salt. Crush into a fine powder with a teaspoon. Heat the vinegar in a small pan until very hot but not boiling. Pour on to the saffron and set aside to infuse for 15 minutes.

Peel the tomatoes: cover with boiling water, quickly stab each tomato with a sharp knife and then drain and skin. Place a sieve over a small bowl. Quarter the tomatoes, remove their seeds and excess pulp and place the seeds and pulp in the sieve. Strain the juice from the seeds and mix into the saffron vinegar. Whisk in 3 tablespoons olive oil, add the basil and season with pepper.

Dice the tomato flesh and mix into the vinaigrette. Cover and chill until needed if wished.

Twist off the prawn heads and discard and peel off their shells. Make a small incision down the length of their backs and remove the dark digestive threads. Rinse clean, pat dry and set aside.

Cook the spaghetti in plenty of boiling salted water according to the packet instructions. This usually takes about 10 minutes. Meanwhile, heat a non-stick frying pan over a high heat. Add 2 tablespoons olive oil and, once hot, fry the prawns briskly, turning regularly, for 3 minutes. Stir in the garlic and chilli and continue to cook for a further minute before adding the drained pasta. Toss thoroughly then mix in the tomato vinaigrette. Adjust the seasoning if necessary and serve immediately.

## SPICED CHRISTMAS CAKE

Don't be discouraged by the length of this recipe, it's actually very easy to make and requires little work other than feeding the cake with lots of rum and Calvados. Some years I don't even marzipan and ice it – it's all a matter of taste and time.

**SERVES ABOUT 12**

170 g currants

170 g sultanas

170 g raisins

130 g stoned prunes, roughly chopped

65 g chopped mixed candied peel

100 g glacé cherries

300 ml dark rum, plus extra for feeding
   the cake

about 95 ml Calvados

255 g plain flour, sifted

³/₄ teaspoon bicarbonate of soda

170 g unsalted butter, softened

170 g dark muscovado sugar

¹/₂ teaspoon ground cinnamon

¹/₂ teaspoon mixed spice

¹/₂ teaspoon ground nutmeg

1 teaspoon Angostura bitters

5 medium eggs, separated

100 ml black treacle

finely grated zest and juice of 1 lemon

finely grated zest of 1 small orange

To ice the cake:

700 g white marzipan

icing sugar for dusting

4 tablespoons redcurrant jelly, warmed

900 g ready-to-roll fondant icing

In a large bowl, mix together the currants, sultanas, raisins, prunes, mixed peel and cherries. Tip into a plastic container that has a lid and mix in 300 ml rum. Seal and leave for a minimum of 2 days. Mix regularly to ensure that all the fruit absorbs the alcohol.

Preheat the oven to Gas Mark ¹/₂/130°C. Lightly grease a 24-cm diameter round cake tin. Then, using the base of your cake tin as a template, cut three circles of greaseproof paper. Place one in the bottom of the tin. Measure the depth of the tin, allow an extra 3 cm in depth and cut a ribbon of greaseproof paper long enough to fit around the inside of the tin. Make a 1 cm deep fold lengthwise down one side and snip into this every 1 cm or so. Press the paper around the side of the tin so that the snipped surface lies flat on the bottom. Now place the second disc of the paper over the first and lightly oil both the lined bottom and sides of the tin. Set aside.

Strain the fruit and measure any remaining sticky rum juice. Add enough Calvados to make up 140 ml and set aside.

Sift the flour, mix in the bicarbonate of soda and set aside. Beat the butter and sugar together until fluffy. Gradually beat in the spices, Angostura bitters and egg yolks, followed by the treacle, grated citrus zest and lemon juice. Mix in half the flour, half the fruit and half the rum-Calvados mixture, then add the remaining fruit, followed by the rest of the flour and the rum and Calvados.

Quickly whisk the egg whites until stiff. Fold into the cake mixture and immediately transfer to the lined cake tin, making sure that there is a slight dip in the middle of the cake. Place in the oven and bake for 3½ hours. After the first 40 minutes, lightly cover the top of the cake with the last paper disc. As all ovens vary slightly in temperature, check to see if the cake is done after the first 2½ hours by inserting a skewer or knife into it. If the skewer comes out clean, the cake is done. Remove from the oven and leave to cool in its tin.

Only remove the cake from the tin when it is completely cold. Peel away the paper before placing on a large clean sheet of foil. Take a fine skewer and puncture the top of the cake. Using a spoon, drizzle in about 3 tablespoons rum. Wrap the cake tightly in the foil and store in an airtight tin. Continue to feed the cake with rum every day or so until you are satisfied that it is sufficiently rich and alcoholic.

To apply the marzipan, turn the cake upside down on a work surface so that its flat bottom becomes the top. Divide the marzipan into two equal portions. Divide one of these in half again and shape into two sausages each approximately half the circumference of the cake. Roll each of these out on a clean surface sprinkled with icing sugar until they are as wide as the cake is high. Now brush the sides of the cake thoroughly with the warmed redcurrant jelly.

Carefully apply the rolled marzipan to the sides of the cake, patting and trimming as necessary. Knead the remaining marzipan into a ball and roll out into a disc large enough to cover the top of the cake. Brush the top of the cake with the redcurrant jelly and gently fit the marzipan over the top of the cake. Leave for a minimum of 3 hours to dry out before icing the cake.

To ice the cake, lightly knead the icing until soft and malleable. Shape it into a large ball and place on a work surface dusted with icing sugar. Shape the ball into a disc and roll it out until you have a large disc about 5 mm thick and 38–43 cm in diameter. Roll the icing by rotating it like the hands of a clock – 5 minutes between every roll of the pin. This should be enough to cover the top and sides of the cake liberally. Brush the marzipan surface with just-boiled water so that it is sticky, then partially roll the icing over the rolling pin and lift it on to the cake. Gently smooth the icing over the top and sides of the cake, smoothing out any pleats as you do so. Trim the bottom of the cake and decorate as you please.

# ICED CINNAMON ROLLS

Be warned – iced cinnamon rolls are very addictive! They convey warm Caribbean breezes, fragrant with frangipani blossom and the scent of freshly brewed coffee.

**MAKES 16 ROLLS**

**150 ml tepid water**

**2 teaspoons dried yeast**

**500 g plain flour**

**1 teaspoon salt**

**50 g caster sugar**

**3 medium egg yolks**

**125 ml full fat milk**

**70 g light muscovado sugar**

**1 tablespoon ground cinnamon**

**4 tablespoons unsalted melted butter, plus extra for greasing**

**For the sticky glaze:**

**170 g icing sugar**

**3–4 tablespoons boiling water**

Measure the tepid water into a small bowl. Sprinkle on the yeast and set aside for 10 minutes or until the yeast has dissolved and smells yeasty and alive.

Mix the flour, salt and caster sugar together in a large bowl. Add the tepid yeast water. Using the yeast water bowl, roughly beat the egg yolks with a fork. Mix the milk into the egg yolks and pour the mixture into the flour. Use your hands to mix everything together until it forms a soft dough. Turn the dough out on to a clean surface and knead thoroughly by repeated stretching and folding under the palm of one hand for 5–10 minutes or until smooth and silky.

Place in clean bowl, cover and leave to rise for 1½ hours or until doubled in size. Mix together the muscovado sugar and the cinnamon.

Turn the dough out on to a clean surface. Knead briefly then roll out into a 30 x 45 cm rectangle. Pour the melted butter on to the dough and brush all over the surface before evenly sprinkling with the cinnamon sugar mixture. Then, starting with the long side, roll the dough into a tight cylinder. Place the seam side down on a flat surface. Trim the edges and cut into 16 slices.

Liberally butter a 20 x 30 cm non-stick baking tray. Arrange the dough slices on the tray, flat side down, in four evenly spaced rows. Cover with cling film.

Heat the oven to Gas Mark 5/190°C. Once it reaches the correct temperature, remove the cling film and bake the buns for 25 minutes or until golden and well risen. They will fuse together as they cook. Remove from the oven and quickly make the sticky icing by gradually mixing 3 or 4 tablespoons of just-boiled water into the icing sugar to make a smooth liquid. Quickly pour over the hot rolls and serve them warm or cold.

## MULLED WINE WITH CARAWAY CHEESE BISCUITS

The smell of warm wine infused with citrus zest and spice is perfect for enhancing the mood of your guests.

**MAKES 6 WINE GLASSES**

**1 bottle claret or robust red wine**

**2 cloves**

**2 blades mace**

**2 allspice berries**

**1 stick cinnamon, broken**

**6 cardamom pods**

**finely pared zest of 1 orange**

**finely pared zest of 1 lemon**

**100 g caster sugar, or to taste**

Pour the wine into a non-corrosive saucepan. Add the cloves, mace, allspice berries, cinnamon stick, cardamom and orange and lemon zest. Set the pan over a low heat and slowly warm the wine to just below boiling point. This will take about 10 minutes. Remove from the heat and leave to infuse for 10–15 minutes. Return to a low heat and, when very hot but not boiling, sweeten to taste. Strain the wine into a punch bowl or jug and serve immediately, preferably with Caraway cheese biscuits (see opposite).

# CARAWAY CHEESE BISCUITS

Spiced savoury biscuits have long been used as an aid to drinking. Apicius Redivivus (Dr. Kitchener) in *The Cook's Oracle* (1818) recommends serving a particularly spicy nibble known as devilled biscuit. This consisted of anchovy paste spiked with mustard, curry powder and/or cayenne pepper and spread over toast. He states it 'frequently makes its appearance at a tavern dinner, when the votaries of Bacchus are determined to vie with each other in sacrificing to the Jolly God.'

These biscuits will keep for a few days in an airtight tin.

---

**MAKES 30 LITTLE BISCUITS**

**115 g plain flour**

**a pinch of salt**

**¼ teaspoon cayenne pepper, or to taste**

**55 g cold unsalted butter, cut into small dice**

**55 g finely grated Parmesan cheese**

**1 medium egg, beaten**

**½ tablespoon caraway seeds**

Preheat the oven to Gas Mark 5/190°C. Sift the flour, salt and cayenne pepper into a large bowl. Rub the butter into the flour until it resembles fine breadcrumbs (or quickly whiz in the food processor and tip into a bowl), then stir in the cheese. Mix in half the egg and about 1 tablespoon cold water. Mix together and turn out on to a floured board.

Lightly knead into a smooth dough and roll out like pastry. Stamp out 5-cm diameter biscuits with a scone cutter. Transfer to a non-stick baking sheet. Lightly re-knead the trimmings, roll out and stamp out more biscuits. Repeat the process until the dough is finished and you have about 30 biscuits.

Prick the biscuits with a fork. Brush with the remaining beaten egg, sprinkle with the caraway seeds and lightly press these into the dough. You can chill for 30 minutes or bake immediately.

Bake for 12 minutes in the preheated oven until golden brown. Remove and cool on a wire cooling rack.

# APPENDIX

This appendix is designed to be useful, hence the recipes for stock and pastry, but I couldn't resist including one of my favourite chocolate cake recipes.

## CHICKEN STOCK

I use all but the breasts of the finest, most flavoursome chicken I can find. Make a large amount, divide it into 500 ml portions and freeze it.

If you want to make a duck stock for the recipe on page 108, buy two oven-ready ducks, remove the breasts and prepare the carcasses as described below. Place the legs, carcasses and wings in a roasting tray and roast at Gas Mark 4/ 200°C in a preheated oven until golden brown. Pour off the excess fat (it's perfect for roast potatoes). Meanwhile, lightly colour the vegetables in the stockpot, then add the browned duck bones and continue as described below.

---

**MAKES 3 LITRES**

**1 large good quality chicken**

**2 tablespoons sunflower oil**

**2 leeks, trimmed white parts only**

**3 large carrots, peeled**

**3 outer sticks celery**

**2 onions, peeled and halved**

**2 cloves garlic, peeled**

**1 bay leaf**

**a few stalks parsley**

**3 peppercorns**

Remove the legs from the chicken and cut each leg in half at the joint. Remove the breasts. Remove the wings from the breasts and cut the wings in half at the joint. The breasts can be set aside or frozen for another recipe. Slice off and discard the parson's nose from the carcass. Cut the carcass in half by going in under the ribs and snapping the spine in two.

Place a large deep saucepan over a medium heat. Mine holds 7 litres of water if filled to the brim. Add the oil and, once hot, start adding the chicken pieces. Brown these on all sides while you prepare the vegetables.

Cut each leek, carrot and celery into three or four pieces. Mix into the chicken with the onions and garlic. Colour lightly and then add enough cold water to come up to the top of the saucepan. Turn the heat to high and skim off the fat as it floats up to the surface. It is crucial to keep skimming during this period. As the water heats up and comes up to the boil it will throw up some scum and more fat. Skim regularly. You may need to top up with more water, depending on how much fat you have to remove. The stock takes about 20 minutes to come up to the boil. As soon as it starts boiling, reduce the heat to a trembling simmer and add the bay leaf, parsley and peppercorns. You shouldn't need to skim once it reaches this stage. Cook very gently for 3 hours. If you let the liquid boil briskly it will turn cloudy. The stock is ready when it tastes good.

Strain the stock through a fine sieve into a large bowl. Ladle it into clean freezer containers. Once cool, chill and then freeze. If possible, set your fridge to quick chill and freezer to fast freeze mode to ensure that the stock cools and freezes quickly.

## SHORTCRUST PASTRY

One of the great myths of modern cooking is that pastry is difficult to make. It isn't. All it requires is confidence, which most of us lack when we're told that a particular task is hard. Homemade pastry has an irresistible buttery flavour that bought pastry can't replicate.

**MAKES 225 G PASTRY (FLOUR WEIGHT)**
**225 g plain flour**
**a pinch of salt**
**115 g cold, firm unsalted butter**

Place the flour and salt in a food processor. Cut the butter into small cubes and add to the flour. Process in short bursts until the mixture forms fine crumbs. Don't over-process into a paste. Tip the crumbs into a mixing bowl. I usually mix in 3 tablespoons cold water with a fork. The quantity of water can vary according to the flour. I usually use organic plain flour. If your dough is too dry and crumbly it will be more crumbly and short when cooked. If your dough is too wet, it will shrink when baked and have a more brittle texture. Nevertheless, both will still taste good. I ightly knead the dough into a ball and roll out as needed. Chill for 30 minutes (or longer if you like) before cooking.

## PUFF PASTRY

For the ultimate buttery flavour, use homemade puff pastry, but only make it when you have plenty of time. The pastry doesn't take long to make, but it needs to be rested regularly in between rollings. The chilling times are the minimum period you should leave the dough, but you can leave it several hours.

**MAKES 225 g PASTRY (FLOUR WEIGHT)**
**225 g plain flour**
**a pinch of salt**
**225 g cold, firm unsalted butter**

Mix together the flour and salt in a food processor. Add 30 g diced cold butter and whiz until it forms fine crumbs. Tip into a bowl and mix in about 125 ml cold water or enough to form a rough dough. Lightly knead into a ball and wrap in a polythene bag. Chill for 30 minutes.

Fifteen minutes before you are ready to roll, take the butter out of the fridge and allow it to soften slightly. Place it between two sheets of cling film and, using a rolling pin, flatten it into a 2.5-cm thick rectangle. Roll out the dough on a floured surface into a rectangle three times the length of the butter and about 2.5 cm wider. Place the butter in the centre and fold over each flap so that the butter is completely covered. With the rolling pin, lightly press on each edge so that the butter is sealed in. Give the dough a half-turn clockwise.

Using short sharp strokes, roll out the dough so that it returns to its previous length (three times that of the butter) but retains the same thickness. Fold over the two ends as before, press the edges with the rolling pin and give a further half-turn clockwise. If the butter is breaking through the pastry or the pastry is becoming warm, stop, wrap and refrigerate for a further 30 minutes. If not, you can repeat the rolling process once more before resting the dough. Make a note of which way the dough is facing before chilling, as you will need to continue with the clockwise half-turns.

After resting the pastry, replace on the floured surface in the same position and continue with a further two rolls and half-turns. Refrigerate for 30 minutes then carry on with two more rolls and half-turns. Wrap and refrigerate or cut in half and freeze.

**And, finally, a sweet note to finish:**

# MINI CHOCOLATE ORANGE CAKES

These cakes taste amazing if you use a really fine flavoured dark chocolate such as Valrhona Caraïbe.

**MAKES 32 BITE-SIZED CAKES**
**115 g dark chocolate**
**55 g unsalted butter, diced**
**3 medium eggs, separated**
**finely grated zest of 2 large oranges**
**85 g caster sugar**
**a pinch of salt**
**20 g plain flour, sifted**
**For the icing and decoration:**
**75 g chocolate**

**60 g unsalted butter, softened**
**1 tablespoon icing sugar**
**zest of 2 oranges, finely julienned**

Preheat the oven to Gas Mark 4/180°C. Put 32 mini paper cake cases on a baking tray.

Break the chocolate into small pieces and place in a bowl that will neatly fit over a saucepan. Half fill the saucepan with just boiled water, but leave off the heat. The chocolate will gently melt. If the water cools too much, replace it with fresh just-boiled water. Once the chocolate is nearly melted, add the butter and stir until it has melted. Remove from the pan of hot water.

Whisk the egg yolks with the orange zest, sugar and salt until fluffy. Add the warm chocolate mixture. Using a metal spoon, fold in the flour. Whisk the egg whites in a clean bowl until they form soft peaks and fold them into the chocolate mixture.

Using a teaspoon, divide the mixture equally between the 32 mini paper cases. Bake in the centre of the oven for about 8 minutes. The cakes should be risen but still moist. You need a little bit of goo inside when you test with a knife. Transfer to a cooling rack and leave until cold.

To make the chocolate butter icing, melt the chocolate as described above. Then, using an electric whisk, beat the butter and icing sugar until fluffy. Whisk in the tepid, melted chocolate. As soon as the cool icing holds its shape, spread it on to the cakes with a knife. Chill until set, then decorate with a few fine strands of orange zest or some gold leaf.

# CONVERSION TABLES

## WEIGHTS

| | | | | | |
|---|---|---|---|---|---|
| 7.5 g | 1/4 oz | 140 g | 5 oz | 795 g | 1 3/4 lb |
| 15 g | 1/2 oz | 170 g | 6 oz | 905 g | 2 lb |
| 20 g | 3/4 oz | 200 g | 7 oz | 1 kg | 2 lb 3 oz |
| 30 g | 1 oz | 225 g | 8 oz | 1.1 kg | 2 1/2 lb |
| 35 g | 1 1/4 oz | 255 g | 9 oz | 1.4 kg | 3 lb |
| 40 g | 1 1/2 oz | 285 g | 10 oz | 1.5 kg | 3 1/2 lb |
| 50 g | 1 3/4 oz | 310 g | 11 oz | 1.8 kg | 4 lb |
| 55 g | 2 oz | 340 g | 12 oz | 2 kg | 4 1/2 lb |
| 65 g | 2 1/4 oz | 370 g | 13 oz | 2.3 kg | 5 lb |
| 70 g | 2 1/2 oz | 400 g | 14 oz | 2.7 kg | 6 lb |
| 80 g | 2 3/4 oz | 425 g | 15 oz | 3.1 kg | 7 lb |
| 85 g | 3 oz | 450 g | 1 lb | 3.6 kg | 8 lb |
| 90 g | 3 1/2 oz | 565 g | 1 1/4 lb | 4.5 kg | 10 lb |
| 115 g | 4 oz | 680 g | 1 1/2 lb | | |

## OVEN TEMPERATURES

| | | | |
|---|---|---|---|
| Very cool | 110°C | 225°F | Gas 1/4 |
| Very cool | 130°C | 250°F | Gas 1/2 |
| Cool | 140°C | 275°F | Gas 1 |
| Slow | 150°C | 300°F | Gas 2 |
| Moderately slow | 170°C | 325°F | Gas 3 |
| Moderate | 180°C | 350°F | Gas 4 |
| Moderately hot | 190°C | 375°F | Gas 5 |
| Hot | 200°C | 400°F | Gas 6 |
| Very hot | 220°C | 425°F | Gas 7 |
| Very hot | 230°C | 450°F | Gas 8 |
| Hottest | 240°C | 475°F | Gas 9 |

## VOLUME

| | | | | | | | | |
|---|---|---|---|---|---|---|---|---|
| 5 ml | | 1 tsp | 85 ml | 3 fl oz | | 225 ml | 8 fl oz | |
| 10 ml | | 1 dsp | 90 ml | | | 240 ml | 8.5 fl oz | |
| 15 ml | 0.5 fl oz | 1 tbsp | 95 ml | | | 255 ml | 9 fl oz | |
| 20 ml | | | 100 ml | 3.5 fl oz | | 270 ml | 9.5 fl oz | |
| 25 ml | | | 105 ml | | | 285 ml | 10 fl oz | 1/2 pint |
| 30 ml | 1 fl oz | | 115 ml | 4 fl oz | | 400 ml | 14 fl oz | |
| 35 ml | | | 120 ml | | | 425 ml | 15 fl oz | 3/4 pint |
| 40 ml | 1.5 fl oz | | 130 ml | 4.5 fl oz | | 565 ml | 20 fl oz | 1 pint |
| 45 ml | | | 140 ml | 5 fl oz | 1/4 pint | 710 ml | 25 fl oz | 1 1/4 pint |
| 50 ml | | | 155 ml | 5.5 fl oz | | 850 ml | 30 fl oz | 1 1/2 pint |
| 55 ml | 2 fl oz | | 170 ml | 6 fl oz | | 1 litre | 35 fl oz | 1 3/4 pint |
| 60 ml | | | 180 ml | | | | | |
| 70 ml | 2.5 fl oz | | 185 ml | 6.5 fl oz | | | | |
| 75 ml | | | 200 ml | 7 fl oz | | | | |
| 80 ml | | | 215 ml | 7.5 fl oz | | | | |

# BIBLIOGRAPHY

Eliza Acton, *Modern Cookery for Private Families* (1855), Southover Press, 1993.

Arabella Boxer, *Book of English Food*, Hodder & Stoughton, 1991.

Edward Bunyard, *The Anatomy of Dessert*, Chatto & Windus, 1933.

Antonio Carluccio, *Complete Mushroom Book The Quiet Hunt*, Quadrille, 2003.

Bernadette Clarke, *The Good Fish Guide*, Marine Conservation Society, 2002.

Elizabeth David, *French Provincial Cooking (1960)*, Grub Street, 2007.

Elizabeth David, *Spices, Salt and Aromatics in the English Kitchen (1970)*, Penguin, 1975.

Elizabeth David, *Summer Cooking (1955)*, Penguin, 1965.

Julie Duff, *Cakes Regional & Traditional*, Grub Street, 2003.

Jane Grigson, *Good Things*, The Cookery Book Club, 1971.

Dorothy Hartley, *Food in England (1954)*, MacDonald, 1964.

Simon Hopkinson with Lindsey Bareham, *Roast Chicken and Other Stories*, Ebury Press, 1994.

Gerhard Jenne, *Decorating Cakes and Cookies*, Ryland, Peters & Small, 1998.

Sybil Kapoor, *Modern British Food*, Penguin, 1996.

Sybil Kapoor, *Simply British*, Penguin, 1999.

Sybil Kapoor, *Taste A New Way to Cook*, Mitchell Beazley, 2003.

Laura Mason with Catherine Brown, *Traditional Foods of Britain, A Regional Inventory*, Prospect Books, 2004.

Harold McGee, *McGee on Food & Cooking*, Hodder & Stoughton, 2004.

Jekka McVicar, *Jekka's Complete Herb Book*, Kyle Cathie, 1994.

Roger Phillips, *Wild Food*, Pan Books, 1983.

Elizabeth Raffald, *The Experienced English Housekeeper*, A. Millar, 1787.

Apicius Redivivus (Dr. Kitchener), *The Cook's Oracle*, John Hatchard, 1818.

Edmund T Rolls, *Emotion Explained*, Oxford University Press, 2005.

Constance Spry & Rosemary Hume, *The Constance Spry Cookery Book (1956)*, Weidenfeld and Nicolson, 1994.

Tom Stobart, *Herbs, Spices and Flavourings (1970)*, Grub Street, 1998.

Shizuo Tsuji, *Japanese Cooking A Simple Art*, Kodansha International, 1985.

J. G. Vaughan and C. A. Geissler, *The New Oxford Book of Food Plants*, Oxford University Press, 1997.

Florence White, *Flowers as Food*, Jonathan Cape, 1934.

Hannah Woolley, *The Gentlewoman's Companion (1675)*, Prospect Books, 2001.

# INDEX